Bilingual

Bilingual

LIFE AND REALITY

François Grosjean

Harvard University Press

Cambridge, Massachusetts, and London, England

First Harvard University Press paperback edition, 2012

Library of Congress Cataloging-in-Publication Data

Grosjean, François.
Bilingual : life and reality / François Grosjean.
p. cm.
Includes bibliographical references and index.
ISBN 978-0-674-04887-4 (cloth : alk. paper)
ISBN 978-0-674-06613-7 (pbk.)
1. Bilingualism. I. Title.
P115.G75 2010 2012
404'.2—dc22   2009043291

To Henri Jean-Baptiste, Caroline, Faith, Jill, and Brigitte,
as well as to Lysiane, Marc, and Eric, who, among many others,
became bilingual unintentionally and live(d) their lives
with two or more languages

Contents

Acknowledgments

I wish to express my gratitude to the many people who have helped me in preparing this book. A very cordial thank you to Elizabeth Knoll, senior editor for behavioral sciences and law at Harvard University Press, who encouraged me to "come back home" for this new book and who has been most helpful at various stages of its preparation. She also very kindly accepted that I use a few carefully chosen extracts from my first book, *Life with Two Languages*. All my thanks to Julie Hagen, who did a wonderful job with the copyediting and with whom I enjoyed working. A few special people took time off to meet with me or to interact extensively with me via e-mail concerning aspects of bilingualism: Elizabeth Beaujour, an expert on bilingual writers; Maria Brisk, a specialist in bilingualism and education; Nancy Huston, a well-established English-French bilingual writer; Olivier Todd, an international journalist and author of biographies; Ellen Bialystok, an expert on the effects of bilingualism in children; Aneta Pavlenko, an authority on various aspects of bilingualism; and Corey Heller, editor of *Multilingual Living Magazine*, who helped me with the list of concerns that parents have when raising bilingual children. To these individuals I should add two anonymous reviewers and a member of the Harvard University Press Board of Syndics, who gave me some very valuable suggestions. May they all receive my heartfelt gratitude.

My thanks also go to those who have sent me their papers (and even books) and who have spoken or written to me. Among them: Cristina Banfi, Veronica Benet-Martinez, John Berry, Philippe Blanchet, Robbins Burling, Susana Chávez-Silverman, Vivian Cook, Tim Cruikshank, Jim Cummins, Susanne Döpke, Nadya Direkova, Karen Emmorey, Lily Wong Fillmore, David Green, John Hale, Michèle Koven, Asaid Khateb, Elizabeth Lanza, David Luna, Stephen Matthews, Teresa McCarty, Elena Nicoladis, Johanne Paradis, Barbara Zurer Pearson, Jennifer Prather (Ariel Dorfman), Paul Preston, Cathy Price, Marie-Eve Perrot, Elliot Roth, Robert Schrauf, Cecilia Serra Stern, Timothy Shanahan, Merrill Swain, Jeanine Treffers-Daller, Jyotsna Vaid, Guadalupe Valdés, Marilyn Vihman, Virginia Yip, Katherine Yoshida, Martine Walsh, Janet Werker, Iwar Werlen, and Jeannie Wurz.

I wish to thank the following for permission to reproduce material in this book: Camilla Cai for excerpts from Einar Haugen, *The Norwegian Language in America: A Study in Bilingual Behavior* (Bloomington: Indiana University Press, 1969), and Einar Haugen, "The Stigmata of Bilingualism," in Anwar Dil, ed., *The Ecology of Language: Essays by Einar Haugen* (Stanford: Stanford University Press, 1972); Harvard University Press for excerpts from François Grosjean, *Life with Two Languages: An Introduction to Bilingualism* (Cambridge, Mass.: Harvard University Press, 1982), copyright © 1982 by the President and Fellows of Harvard College; McArthur & Company for excerpts from Nancy Huston, *Losing North: Musings on Land, Tongue and Self* (Toronto: McArthur & Company, 2002), copyright © 2002 by McArthur & Company.

Finally, my deep gratitude goes to my immediate family, Lysiane, Marc, and Eric, who have been wonderful in their support over the years and so interesting to interact with when discussing, among other things, our lives with two or more languages in several cultures.

Introduction

As I sit down to work on this book, I marvel at people who are bilingual—that is, who use two or more languages in their everyday life. In the span of a few hours this Monday morning, I bought croissants in French from the baker's wife, who then served the next client in Swiss German; I accompanied my bilingual wife into town to meet her trilingual Italian-French-German friend; I stopped by my garage to have my car checked by a mechanic of Italian origin, who explained to me, in French, how the cooling system worked. While going from one place to another, I listened to the radio and heard that the former long-time Colombian hostage Ingrid Betancourt had spent her Sunday in Paris with French friends and had spoken in Spanish, on Colombia's Caracol Radio, to the hostages who had not been freed along with her. I also listened to Roger Federer in London, talking about the final he had played at Wimbledon; he was tired, having finished his game against Rafael Nadal quite late in the evening and then given interviews in his four different languages (Swiss German, German, French, and English). Now, as I am settling down at my desk, accompanied by the music of George Frideric Handel, a German-Italian-English trilingual, I can hear the children in the day-care center across the street singing songs in French and Italian. Bilingualism is indeed present in practically every country in the world, in all classes of society, in all age groups. It has been estimated that half of the world's population, if not more, is bilingual. This book is about them.

Why a new book after so many others on the same topic? The reason goes back a long way. When I was a young student at the University of Paris coming to terms with my own bilingualism and biculturalism, I looked for a book on the subject and found only scholarly works that were rather long and difficult to read (I wasn't a linguist then). In addition, I didn't feel that they addressed the very down-to-earth issues I was interested in at that moment, nor did they answer some of my basic questions: What is bilingualism? Was I really a bilingual? Why was I suddenly having difficulties with language when things had gone smoothly until that point? (I had just returned to France after a ten-year absence.) Was I English, as my education had made me, or French, as my name and my passport indicated? Was it all right to be bicultural? These were some of the questions I was seeking answers to, and looking back over the years, I now know that many bilinguals have asked themselves the same questions. It took me quite some time, and my own delving into bilingualism, first at the level of my master's thesis and then as a researcher in my own right, to come to satisfactory answers.

More than forty years later, after publishing my books *Life with Two Languages* and *Studying Bilinguals* and many scholarly papers, I felt the need to write the simple, basic introduction I had been looking for as a young man. Admittedly, there are numerous introductory textbooks on bilingualism (I am the author of one), there are edited volumes and more specialized monographs, there is an encyclopedia on the topic, and there are academic journals (I helped found one), not to mention newsletters for bilingual families and numerous Web sites dedicated to the subject. That said, even though the phenomenon is widespread, bilingualism as a topic is still unfamiliar to most people. In addition, bilingualism is surrounded by a number of myths: bilinguals are rare and have equal and perfect knowledge of their languages; real bilinguals have acquired their two or more languages in childhood and have no accent in either of them; bilinguals are born translators; switching between languages is a sign of laziness in bilinguals; all bilinguals are also bicultural; bilinguals have double or split personalities; bilingualism will delay language acquisition in children and have negative effects on their development; if you want your child to grow up bilingual, use the one person–one language approach; children being raised bilingual will always mix their languages; and so on.

My first aim in this book is to present the various facets of being bilingual as simply and as clearly as possible and, while doing so, to demystify who bilinguals are. Unlike with my more scholarly writings on the topic, I have a very general readership in mind here, made up of those who are interested in bilingualism or involved, in one way or another, with bilinguals: general readers and students, parents planning to raise or already raising bilingual children, spouses and members of extended families who interact with bilinguals, as well as colleagues and friends, and professionals who deal with bilingual children, such as teachers, psychologists, and speech therapists. My second aim—as important as the first—is to offer bilinguals a book about who they are, written by someone who is himself bilingual and who has been through the highs and lows of living with several languages and cultures. Many bilinguals do not consider themselves to be bilingual and are critical of their own language competence. I hope that this book will help them come to terms with their own reality and accept who they are—competent but different types of users of languages.

I want this book to be optimistic but also realistic. Bilingualism is not the burden or the problem it has been made out to be by some, but neither is it the complete bliss that others would have us believe. Bilingualism is quite simply a fact of life for millions and millions of people, with its ups and downs, its good times and its bad times, its moments of joy (there are many) and its moments of frustration (there are some). As a bilingual and bicultural person myself, I will try to describe people who, like me, know and use several languages and interact with different cultures; I will try do so in as clear and informative a way as possible.

This book has two parts: the first concerns bilingual adults and the second bilingual children. Each part is broken down into short chapters that discuss various aspects of the bilingual person. In Part I, I examine the reasons why people are bilingual and show the extent of bilingualism. I then describe bilinguals in terms of language fluency and use, and look at the different functions of the bilingual's languages. I spend three chapters on how bilinguals adapt their language production to the situation and to those they are interacting with—other bilinguals or monolinguals—and I cover such bilingual behaviors as code-switching, borrowing, and interference. I then devote a chapter to what it means to have an accent in one or several languages, something that is in fact quite normal when one is bilingual. I continue with the bilingual's languages across the lifespan—that is, how the knowledge and use of different languages wax and wane, depending on changing need. The next chapter examines the attitudes and feelings that bilinguals, and also monolinguals, have toward bilingualism. It is followed by a chapter on biculturalism, a phenomenon that is not automatically linked to bilingualism but impinges on the life of many bilinguals. This is followed by a discussion of the personality of bilinguals, how thinking and dreaming take place in bilinguals, and how they express their emotions with one or all of their languages. The final two chapters in Part 1 deal with bilingual writers and other "special" bilinguals. Over the years, I have described and championed regular, everyday bilinguals. I continue to do so in this book, as they make up the great majority of bilinguals. But I have decided also to evoke special, sometimes exceptional, bilinguals: language teachers, translators and interpreters, well-known people who are bilingual, even secret agents, as well as bilingual authors who write literature in their second language or in both their languages, an outstanding feat.

In Part 2, I explain how children can go in and out of bilingualism very rapidly and how this depends largely on the need they have for the languages they are in contact with. I then discuss the ways of becoming bilingual as a child: two languages are acquired simultaneously in infancy, or one language is acquired in infancy, followed by a second language at some later time. I follow this with a chapter on linguistic aspects of childhood bilingualism, addressing dominance in a language, adapting to the language mode, language "mixing," bilingual children as interpreters, and the way bilingual children play with languages. I spend a chapter discussing the strategies families can adopt to ensure that their children become bilingual, and the support that they, and their children, should receive to maintain the family's languages. A chapter on the effects of bilingualism on children's development addresses a question on the minds of many parents. I cover the problems of past bilingualism studies and where the research stands today, and also say a few words about bilingual children and language disorders. In the final chapter I discuss education and bilingualism and review programs in which the educational aim is not bilingualism, as well as those where bilingualism is one of the goals.

What are the differences between this new book and *Life with Two Languages*? First, this book is shorter and covers only certain aspects of bilingualism, concentrating on the adult and the child. Political, demographic, and social aspects of bilingualism, for example, are not dealt with here. Second, this book is written so as to be accessible to a large general readership and not mainly to students and professionals. Hence the shorter chapters, the far fewer references made to the research literature, and the reduced emphasis on domains—some of them my own—such as the cognitive and neurolinguistic aspects of bilingualism, or the modeling of bilingual processing. Third, more than twenty-five years have passed since *Life with Two Languages* was published, and my thinking on a few topics has evolved. In sum, I would say that the two books are good companions to each other. The reader who has finished this book and is interested in knowing more may want to pick up the earlier work, which covers more domains, is certainly more exhaustive, and offers many more personal testimonies from bilinguals themselves.

As in *Life with Two Languages,* I let bilinguals speak for themselves about their personal experiences as people who live with two or more languages and cultures. I also present a few short extracts from the works of bilingual authors, including Eva Hoffman, Nancy Huston, Richard Rodriguez, and Olivier Todd, because their talent as writers allows them to express in just the right words feelings about, and experiences of, bilingualism that many of us have shared.

The scholarly references I cite in this volume span several decades, although the majority are quite recent. Why such a large time span, and why some older references? The answer is simple. The study of bilingualism now has a long history, and it is important to mention the classic works of some of the early researchers in the field, such as Einar Haugen, Uriel Weinreich, William Mackey, Wallace Lambert, and others. They set the stage for scholars of my generation, and for the ones following mine. That said, I do not actually cite many references in this text, as I do not want to weigh down the chapters with notes. Readers who want to delve further into particular aspects of bilingualism may refer to my previous works, as well as to the many other introductory and more advanced books on the subject.

I

Bilingual Adults

I

Why Are People Bilingual?

Out of curiosity, I googled the word "bilingual" and came up with more than 32 million hits (a number that will have increased by the time you read this). I then looked up the ways the word was used and found it in the contexts of bilingual dictionaries, bilingual professions, bilingual people, bilingual laws, bilingual nations, bilingual books, bilingual toys, bilingual studies, bilingual ballots, bilingual databases, bilingual schools, and so on. As I went through the list (I gave up after a few pages), it became clear that the word "bilingual" was being used in many different ways, such as, "who know and use two languages" (in reference to bilingual people), "which are presented in two languages" (bilingual books, ballots), "which need two languages" (bilingual professions), "which recognize two languages" (bilingual nations), or "which go from one language to the other" (bilingual dictionaries). It also emerged that some expressions are not clear. Is a bilingual school, for example, a school that welcomes and caters to two monolingual language populations, a school that uses two languages in its teaching, or a school that promotes bilingualism in its children? The take-home message from this is that we must be careful in interpreting the word "bilingual" when we see it or hear it.

In this book matters will be simpler, as we will be concentrating on bilingual adults and bilingual children. In addition, I propose this definition of bilinguals at the outset:

Bilinguals are those who use two or more languages (or dialects) in their everyday lives.

Three points need to be made with regard to this definition. First, it puts the emphasis on the regular use of languages and not on fluency, as I shall discuss in more detail in Chapter 2. Second, it includes dialects along with languages. Thus, an Italian who uses one of Italy's many dialects, such as Pugliese, as well as Italian is considered to be bilingual, just as a person who uses English and Spanish on a regular basis is. Third, the definition includes two or more languages, since some people use three or four languages, if not more.

I have often been asked why I don't use the word "multilingual." Two reasons come to mind. The first is that some people are "only" bilingual (they know and use two languages) and it seems odd to use the term "multilingual" when describing them. The second is that the word "multilingual" is used less than "bilingual" in reference to individuals. There is a long tradition in the field of extending the notion of bilingualism to those who use two or more languages on a regular basis.

Before spending several chapters examining the bilingual person, we need to ask ourselves why people are bilingual and why it is that so many inhabitants of the world use two or more languages in their everyday life. In this chapter we will look first at the factors that lead to bilingualism, and second at how extensive bilingualism really is.

Reasons That Lead to Bilingualism

If you attempt to find out the number of languages there are in the world, you will come up with many different answers. A primary reason for this is how you define a language as compared with a variety of a language, often called a dialect. When you include each dialect as an independent language, the count goes up; when you don't, the number goes down. The Web site and reference book *Ethnologue: Languages of the World* presents a comprehensive catalogue of all the known living languages in the world today. It basically applies the criteria of mutual intelligibility between dialects and a common literature to determine whether two dialects are part of the same language, but it also allows for exceptions based on ethnolinguistic identities. According to the latest count by *Ethnologue,* close to 7,000 languages exist in the world (the exact number in the 2005 edition is 6,912 languages). The area with the fewest languages is Europe (only 239 languages) and the area with the most languages is Asia (2,269). One outstanding area, which we all tend to see as vast but devoid of important land masses—and hence of languages—is the Pacific, but in fact as many as 1,310 languages are spoken on the various islands scattered across the great expanse of the Pacific Ocean.[1]

With so many languages in the world (even though, according to *Ethnologue,* some 516 of them are nearly extinct), a lot of contact is bound to take place between people of different language groups. And with such language contact, bilingualism will arise. Members of one group will learn the language of another—just as, for instance, Swiss Germans learn French, or immigrants to the United States learn English. Sometimes the learning is reciprocal, although this is rare. Other times, interacting groups will learn a lingua franca (a language of communication), such as Swahili, which is used for between-group interaction in Eastern Africa.

Let us now look more closely at the reasons for language contact and bilingualism.

Linguistic Makeup of a Country

A rather rough way of assessing the amount of language contact that takes place in each country is to divide the number of languages in the world (some 7,000) by the number of countries (192, according to the United Nations at the time of writing). The result, an average of 36 languages per country, gives us some idea of the extent of linguistic diversity. According to linguist William Mackey, however, this figure requires a few correctives. First, Mackey points out, some languages are numerically more significant than others. *Ethnologue* estimates that 94 percent of the world's people speak 347 languages, or approximately 5 percent of all the languages. Among the languages spoken by the most people we find Mandarin Chinese, Spanish, English, Bengali, Hindi/Urdu, Arabic, Portuguese, Russian, Japanese, and French. Second, some languages are spoken natively in several countries (for example, Spanish is spoken throughout Central and South America, English in many Commonwealth countries). That said, many countries are home to numerous languages: there are some 516 languages in Nigeria, according to *Ethnologue,* 427 in India, 275 in Australia, 200 in Brazil, 280 in Cameroon, and so on. In fact, it is difficult to find countries with only one or two languages; they are usually isolated geographically (islands such as Greenland and Saint Helena) or politically (North Korea, Cuba).[2]

Linguistic contact within a country, and hence bilingualism, will depend on many factors. One is language distribution within the country. If the distribution is geographically based—that is, if the various languages are found in specific areas—there may be less contact than if the language groups all occupy the same territory. One example with which I am very familiar is Switzerland, where the linguistic borders between the four national languages are relatively well delineated: French is spoken in the west, Italian basically in the Ticino area (central southern tip of the country), Romansh in a small area in the eastern part of the country, and German in the rest of the territory. Invariably bilingualism occurs all along the linguistic borders (I live some three miles from the French-German border) and also in border towns like Fribourg and Biel/Bienne. In other countries, two or more languages occupy the same territory (for instance, English and Spanish in the American Southwest), and in such cases the chances of bilingualism are greater, all other things being equal, since much more contact takes place between groups.

Another factor is the language policy of the country. If a government recognizes several languages and gives them some official status (as Canada does with English and French, and Belgium with French, Flemish, and German), then the language contact may not be as great as in countries that recognize one official language among the many that are spoken. In the case of Belgium, for example, some contact occurs between the indigenous language groups and each group learns the language of the others in school, but many people lead their lives in basically one language. In contrast, when a country has just one national language (recognized or not), or an accepted lingua franca, as in many African nations, then members of most language groups have to become bilingual (examples would be the Inuit in Canada, the Navajo in the United States, the Kabyles in Algeria, the Albanians in Greece, the Hungarians in Romania, the Finns in Sweden, and so forth). Of course, other factors will have some influence, such as the linguistic and education policies of a country and the attitudes vis-à-vis different language groups. A Belgian offers this assessment of the linguistic situation in his country:

> Every child at school learns both languages starting in early primary school. Flemish-speaking people . . . learn and know French much better, because French is a much more useful and international language.[3]

Movement of Peoples

In today's world, in addition to language contact between indigenous groups, contact occurs between the indigenous groups and speakers of other languages who have immigrated to that region or country. Several patterns may lead to bilingualism. Most frequently, at least nowadays, the immigrants (to the United States, England, or France, for instance) learn the language of their new homeland, but the indigenous population may also learn the language of the settlers (thus, historically we find American Indians learning English in the United States, and Egyptians learning Arabic during the Arab settlement of Egypt). In some cases, but rarely, each group learns the language of the other (as when Spanish settlers in Paraguay learned Guaraní and Guaraní Indians learned Spanish).

People have always moved within and across countries and continents and have done so for many different reasons. Trade, commerce, and business have long given rise to language contact and hence bilingualism. In earlier times, when traders traveled to areas where another language was spoken or a lingua franca was used, many—buyers as well as sellers—became bilingual. Greek was the lingua franca of trade in the Mediterranean during the third, fourth, and fifth centuries BCE. Today, Russian is the language of trade and business throughout Russia and the nations of the former Soviet Union (more than a hundred languages are spoken in the Russian Federation), and of course English is a major language of trade and business throughout the world. Business today increasingly operates on global dimensions. Many people move to another country for a few years to work for an international division of their company; their families often accompany them, and both adults and children may become bilingual. And we should note here that it is not always necessary for people to migrate physically for language contact to take place. A great many businesspeople communicate with each other by phone and online, in English and other international languages, across countries and time zones, and then return to their normal, often monolingual, lives at the end of the workday.

People also move around the world for political and religious reasons. World history is full of examples of people moving to another land and, more often than not, another language, for political reasons: Russians migrated after the 1917 Revolution, Sudeten Germans after World War II, Cubans during the Castro era, Vietnamese after the fall of South Vietnam. As for religious migrations, Huguenot Protestants fled France after the revocation of the Edict of Nantes in 1685 and settled in Russia, England, Holland, and America, for example. In the twentieth century Russian Jews left the Soviet Union under difficult circumstances and settled in Israel or the

United States, among other countries. And in recent years, many Christians have been leaving the Middle East and resettling elsewhere.

Even though military invasions, wars, and colonization are probably less frequent today than in the past, they have been the cause of much language contact. Alexander the Great and his armies spread Greek throughout the Middle East; the Roman Empire brought Latin to much of Europe, North Africa, and the Middle East; the Spanish conquistadores in the Americas spread their language; colonizations in the nineteenth century increased the number of speakers of French, English, and Russian, and so on.

Finally, migration for economic and social reasons is a major factor in the movement of peoples and hence of language contact. People have always moved to other regions, countries, or continents in search of work and better living conditions. Many countries throughout the world have a history of immigration, and many, such as Australia, Canada, the United States, Brazil, and Argentina, have been built on this very phenomenon. Western Europe, which many left in earlier centuries for better conditions elsewhere, has now, in turn, become home to large immigrant communities that are in various stages of integration.

Within the first few generations of immigration, there is a great deal of language contact as immigrants and their descendants continue to speak their native language and also, most of the time, the language(s) of their new country. It has been estimated, for example, that owing to immigration, some 300 different languages are spoken in London today, and that even a small market town like Boston in Lincolnshire, England, with a population of 70,000, houses some 65 spoken languages.[4]

Education and Culture

Education and culture have always been and will always be domains in which outside languages are learned and used. As far back as the time of the Roman Empire, almost all educated Romans learned Greek, which was the language of medicine, rhetoric, philosophy, and so on. Later in Europe, Italian and then French took on the same role, as did German for scientific domains in the nineteenth century. Today, English has taken over as the main lingua franca of education and culture. In addition, millions of children and students, in many different countries, not only learn one or two languages as subjects in school but are also educated in a language that is not their native language. This is the case, for example, in numerous African and Asian nations as well as in most immigration countries. A Marathi-Hindi-English trilingual writes:

> When I first went to school I did not know English, but I
> started English as a subject in secondary school, and
> then English was the medium of instruction at college.[5]

A Farsi-English bilingual says:

> I did not know how to speak English until I was ten
> years old, when I went to an English-speaking school in
> Tehran.[6]

Some schoolchildren and older students may actually travel some distance to be schooled or to go to college in a different language. An example close to my home is seen in the French border area where I live in Switzerland. There is a long-established tradition among Swiss German students of crossing the linguistic border to attend our local French-speaking high school instead of going to their own German-speaking high school. We often hear the students chatting away in Swiss German as they walk from the train station, and by the end of their schooling they have become German-French bilinguals. As for college, one need only think of all the students who travel to France, Russia, the United Kingdom, the United States, and elsewhere, to obtain a degree. These students become active bilinguals very quickly.

Other Factors

Among other factors leading to bilingualism, three come to mind: bilingual families, people's professions, and deafness. Concerning the first, there are innumerable bilingual households in which the children learn the home language (or home languages) as well as the language(s) outside the home. We will come back to this in Part 2 of this book, but this is a very common way of becoming bilingual. Here is the testimony of one English-Spanish bilingual:

> I was born and grew up in Colombia, South America. In the type of family environment I was brought up in, hearing and speaking two languages [Spanish and English] was a normal thing. My mother is Canadian and my father Colombian, and each would speak to us in their respective native language.[7]

Second is the simple fact that certain jobs require the knowledge and use of several languages. We have already mentioned trade, commerce, and various financial businesses. Many other professions need people to know two or more languages as well: tourism and travel, the hotel and restaurant industry, diplomacy, research, the media (including foreign reporting), show business, language teaching and bilingual education, interpreting and translation, aid to developing countries, and so on. Today's workplace is very often bilingual, if not multilingual.

Third, being hard of hearing or deaf often leads to bilingualism in the language of the majority group (English in the United States, for example) and the sign language of the Deaf community that exists in the country or region (American Sign Language in the United States, for instance).[8]

The Extent of Bilingualism

Based on this discussion of the wide extent of bilingualism, one wonders what has given rise to the following misconception:

Myth: Bilingualism is a rare phenomenon.

This false impression probably comes from the fact that one rarely has an overall view of the amount of language contact that occurs in the world. It may also be that some people have very restricted definitions of what it means to be bilingual (we will come back to this in the next chapter). What is certain is that bilingualism is present in practically every country of the world, in all classes of society, in all age groups.

So how many bilinguals are there? Even though I have worked in the field for many years, I still haven't found a good answer. Like many others, I have reported that half of the world's population, if not more, is bilingual. But the data we all would like to have are missing. This is because counting the number of users of a single language is already very difficult (see the problem of separating a dialect from a language) and also because surveys and censuses do not agree on what questions to ask. Should individuals be asked which languages they know, which they use, which they spoke as a child? In addition, bilingualism and biculturalism are sometimes seen as phenomena that "dilute" a linguistic or cultural group (does the bilingual/bicultural person belong to group A or group B?) and hence it is easier to ask simple, one-language and one-culture questions.

That said, there are some data around that we can use. For example, the European Commission published a report in 2006 that asked Europeans about their mother tongue and their knowledge of other languages. To the question concerning which languages (excluding the mother tongue) people spoke well enough to be able to have a conversation, 56 percent of those polled (in twenty-five different countries) named one other language, thus indicating their potential bilingualism (even if they did not speak the two languages on a daily basis), and 28 percent named a third language (making them potentially trilingual). So slightly more than half of Europe's population is probably at least bilingual. As would be expected, the countries with the most bilinguals are primarily the smaller ones: Luxembourg, Slovakia, Latvia, The Netherlands, Slovenia—to which we should add Switzerland, which was not included in the poll as it is not officially a member of the European Union. The more monolingual countries are primarily the larger ones, such as Great Britain—where, nevertheless, 38 percent of those polled reported being able to speak at least one language other than their mother tongue.[9]

How about North America? Let's begin with Canada. Statistics Canada reports that slightly more than 5 million people claimed in Canada's 2001 census that they were bilingual in English and

French, an 8.1 percent increase over the number five years earlier. They represent almost 18 percent of the population. As would be expected, almost half of the Francophones are bilingual, as opposed to only 9 percent of the Anglophones. In addition, another 18 percent of the population reports having some mother tongue other than English and French; since most of those individuals probably also use one of the two national languages, the bilingual population of Canada is therefore probably around 35 percent, a percentage somewhat lower than Europe's.[10]

What is the situation in the United States? More than thirty years ago, in *Life with Two Languages*, I analyzed the 1976 Survey of Income and Education. It had asked language questions of those who reported a non-English background in the household. I worked out then that a bit fewer than 13 million inhabitants (some 6 percent of the population) reported speaking both English and a minority language on a regular basis—that is, they were bilingual. I concluded that the United States was a heavily monolingual country when compared with other countries of the world.[11] Since then, the U.S. censuses have asked which language is spoken at home other than English and how well the person speaks English. Close to 18 percent of the population in the 2000 census reported speaking another language at home, up from 14 percent in 1990 and 11 percent in 1980. Of the almost 47 million who reported using another language, close to 36 million reported that they spoke English very well or well, which would mean that some 13.71 percent of the total U.S. population was bilingual. If we add those who reported speaking English "not well," the overall percentage of bilinguals increases to close to 17 percent.[12] If one adds the many Americans who use a second or third language outside the home and who weren't counted as other language users in the censuses, we certainly have an increase in the proportion of bilinguals in the United States. The numbers do not reach those of Europe, not to mention those in many Asian and African nations, but the United States is certainly a country with many bilinguals—an estimated 55 million in 2009!

As for the languages spoken in the United States along with English, by far the most-used language, according to the 2000 census, is Spanish (some 28 million speakers, an increase of 10 million between 1990 and 2000).[13] Following Spanish, in the top ten one finds several Asian languages (Chinese, Tagalog, Korean, Vietnamese) as well as "old" European languages (French, German, Italian, Russian, Polish). The latter, with the exception of Russian, have lost speakers compared with the past. It should be noted that a number of languages that were in the top ten in the middle of the twentieth century, such as Yiddish and the Scandinavian languages, had fallen off strongly by 2000. For example, the number of Yiddish speakers had gone from 1.7 million in 1940 to fewer than 200,000 in 2000 (and it was mainly being spoken by elderly individuals).

In sum, bilingualism is a worldwide phenomenon, found on all continents and in the majority of the countries of the world. In some, such as the Asian and African countries for which we unfortunately do not have good data, the percentages found in Europe and North America are most probably surpassed. As a Luganda-Swahili-English speaker writes concerning Uganda:

> Everybody in my country is encouraged to speak as many
> languages as he or she can master. As a bilingual I find
> that I can relate to a wide range of people who come
> from different parts of Uganda.[14]

An Akan-Fanti-English trilingual from Ghana says:

> People take pride in being bilingual because they are gen-
> erally looked upon with respect. Some of the languages
> are dominant, and being able to speak them is a great ad-
> vantage. Ghana really encourages bilingualism . . . My ex-
> perience as a bilingual is a great one. This is because I
> have been able to communicate freely and with ease with
> others who are not my kinsmen.[15]

2

Describing Bilinguals

One day, I was sitting at an outdoor café and over-heard three people talking about what it means to be bilingual. I pricked up my ears but resisted the temptation to interrupt, even though they were talking about my pet subject. One of them insisted that being bilingual meant being totally fluent in two languages; another agreed and added that the bilingual person also had to have grown up with both languages. The third person was less assertive and mentioned simply the regular use of two languages. "After all," she asked, "someone might know two languages fluently but almost never use one of them; does that make him bilingual? What about the person who doesn't know the two languages to the same level but who uses them regularly? Isn't she bilingual?" I sipped my coffee quietly at the next table and promised myself that in my next book on bilingualism I would write a chapter on this very issue.

Below, in addition to examining the criteria of fluency and use, we will look at some other factors that help characterize bilinguals, such as which languages they use and what they use them for, what their language history is, their proficiency in the various linguistic skills, the language modes they navigate in, and whether they are also bicultural.

Language Fluency or Language Use?

A number of years ago, I asked some monolingual college students what they understood me to mean when I told them that person X was bilingual in English and French. The top answer (from 36 percent of the students) was that it meant X speaks both languages fluently. When asked to rate the importance of fluency on a 1 to 5 scale, where 1 was not important and 5 very important, they gave "fluent in two languages" a high mean rating of 4.7.

The notion that being bilingual means being fluent in your languages is widespread. The bilingual writer Nancy Huston, who is Canadian but has lived in France for many years, has given much thought to her dual language and cultural status and has written about it. I will mention her views in several parts of this book. For Huston, true bilinguals are those who learn to master two languages in early childhood and who can move back and forth between them smoothly and effortlessly.[1] Even some linguists have put forward fluency as the defining characteristic of bilinguals. The American linguist Leonard Bloomfield, for example, wrote that bilingualism was the native-like control of two languages.[2] Several decades later, the lecturer and diplomatic interpreter Christophe Thiery set the bar very high when he wrote,

> A true bilingual is someone who is taken to be one of
> themselves by the members of two different linguistic
> communities, at roughly the same social and cultural
> level.[3]

He reported that the "true" bilinguals he studied had learned their languages in their youth (before age fourteen), had spoken both languages at home, had gone back and forth between the two language communities, and had been taught in both their languages.

In addition, they had no accent in either language, they were equally fluent in all the skills of their two languages, and they did not let one language interfere with the other when speaking to monolinguals.

A major aim of this book will be to show that the majority of bilinguals simply do not resemble these rare individuals. While a few may, such as interpreters and translators (and we will turn to them in the chapter on "special bilinguals"), most bilinguals are simply not like that. They may not have acquired their languages in childhood, spoken their languages in the home, or lived in two-language communities. Many have not been schooled in all their languages, many have an accent in one of their languages, and more often than not one language does interfere with the other. If one were to count as bilingual only those who can pass as monolinguals in each language, one would have no label for the vast majority of people who use two or more languages regularly but do not have native-like fluency in each. According to the fluency definition, they are not bilingual, and yet they are not monolingual either, because they live their lives with more than one language.

The monolingual view of bilingualism that one still finds in the general public (but much less often among specialists in bilingualism) has led to a common misapprehension:

Myth: Bilinguals have equal and perfect knowledge of their languages.

Some add that bilinguals must have acquired their languages as children, and some others bring in the idea that they should not have an accent in any of them. These are the "real," the "pure," the "balanced," the "perfect" bilinguals. All the others (in fact, the majority of people who use two or more languages in their everyday life) are viewed as "not really" or "less" bilingual. One consequence of this is that the language skills of bilinguals have almost always been appraised in terms of monolingual standards. The effects of bilingualism have been closely scrutinized, and bilinguals themselves rarely evaluate their language competencies as adequate. They have a tendency to assume and amplify the monolingual view of bilingualism and thus criticize their own bilingualism. They complain that they don't speak one of their languages well, that they have an accent, that they mix their languages, and so on. Many do not want to be labeled bilingual, and some even hide their knowledge of their weaker language.

All this is unfortunate, as it does not take into account the reality, which we will discuss in more depth in the next chapter, that most bilinguals use their languages for different purposes, in different situations, with different people. They simply do not need to be equally competent in all their languages. The level of fluency they attain in a language (more specifically, in a language skill) will depend on their need for that language and will be domain specific. Hence, many bilinguals are dominant in one language, some do not know how to read and write one of their languages, and others have only passive knowledge of a language. Perhaps a sprinkling of bilinguals may have equal and perfect fluency in their languages, although Einar Haugen—one of the fathers of bilingualism research, whom I had the honor of knowing—did not believe this was truly possible. He wrote:

> Is it possible to keep the patterns of two (or more) languages absolutely pure, so that a bilingual in effect becomes two monolinguals, each speaking one language perfectly but also perfectly understanding the other and able to reproduce in one the meaning of the other with-

out at any point violating the usage of either language?
On the face of it one is inclined to say no. Hypothetically
it is possible just as a perfectly straight line or perfect
beauty or perfect bliss are theoretically possible, but in
practice it is necessary to settle for less.[4]

Because defining bilinguals in terms of language fluency is problematic, many researchers have opted for language *use* as the defining criterion, and little by little an increasing number of bilinguals are adopting it when describing their own bilingualism. Uriel Weinreich and William Mackey, two important scholars who marked the field of bilingualism in the second half of the last century, both leaned in this direction. They defined bilingualism as the alternate use of two (or more) languages.[5] My own definition—bilinguals are those who use two or more languages (or dialects) in their everyday lives—is very similar and also puts the stress on language use.

The range of who can be considered bilingual increases considerably when one concentrates on language use. At one end we find the migrant worker who may speak with some difficulty the host country's language and who does not read and write it. At the other end, we have the professional interpreter who is fully fluent in two languages. In between, we find the scientist who reads and writes articles in a second language but who rarely speaks it, the foreign-born spouse who interacts with friends in his first language, the member of a linguistic minority who uses the minority language only at home and the majority language in all other domains of life, the Deaf person who uses sign language with her friends but a spoken language (often in its written form) with a hearing person, and so on. Despite the great diversity among these people, they all share a common feature: they lead their lives with two or more languages.

Language Fluency and Language Use

Despite the increasing emphasis put on language use when describing bilinguals, one cannot do away with the notion of fluency—that is, which languages bilinguals know and the degree of proficiency they have in them. I have developed a grid, shown in Figure 2.1, that takes into account both factors.

Language use is presented along the grid's vertical axis by a continuum (from "never" used to "daily" use), and language fluency is presented along the horizontal axis ("low" fluency to "high" fluency). A bilingual's languages can be placed on the grid according

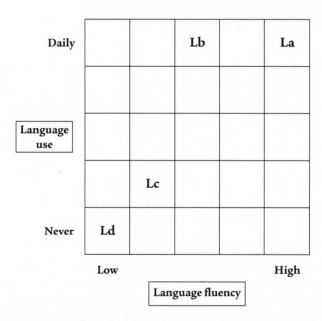

Figure 2.1. Describing the bilingual in terms of language use and language fluency. The languages in this example are English (La), Spanish (Lb), Italian (Lc), and French (Ld).

to the levels reached in each dimension. In the example given, I depict the bilingualism of Ana, a second-year chemistry major at a large midwestern university. Because of her background (her parents emigrated from the Dominican Republic), the year she spent abroad in Italy, and the languages she studied at school, she has four languages: La (English), Lb (Spanish), Lc (Italian), and Ld (French). She has high fluency in La (English) and medium fluency in Lb (Spanish), both of which she uses daily. She has rather low fluency in Lc (Italian), which she uses irregularly with an Italian girlfriend she met in Italy (the friend knows three of Ana's languages), and low fluency in Ld (French), which she never uses. (Interested readers might wish to fill in the grid with their own languages according to their use and fluency levels.)

The older definition of bilingualism puts the emphasis on high language fluency (the right-hand part of the grid). Since our example bilingual, Ana, has medium fluency in Lb, she might not have been counted as a bilingual according to that view. The more recent definition of bilingualism puts the emphasis on regular language use (top part of the grid); we see that Ana uses both La and Lb on a daily basis and so can be considered bilingual. Whether Ana is trilingual (in La, Lb, and Lc) depends on where the border is drawn on the language-use continuum. At first glance, we could say that she is bilingual in languages La and Lb and has some knowledge of Lc and Ld. This pattern is common in today's world: bilinguals may use two or more languages on a regular basis and also have some knowledge of one or more other languages.

In this book I will often address the issue of which languages a bilingual *knows*, even if it is with a very low level of fluency, and which languages he or she *uses*. I will do so by referring back to this grid.

Making Things a Bit More Complex

Many other factors—in addition to traditional biographical data (age, sex, socioeconomic status, occupation, and so on)—need to be taken into account when describing bilinguals. I will mention a few here and take some of them up again in later chapters.

First, as indicated in Figure 2.1, we need to know which languages bilinguals actually know and which they use. Many of us know several languages to varying degrees (in my case, the number is four) but we use fewer than that on a regular basis (in my case the number is two). We also need to know what the relationship is between the languages a person uses. This will help us understand the influence that one language can have on the other (languages that are closer to one another, for example, have a tendency to influence one another more).

It is also important to know whether some languages are still being acquired (think of someone who has been in the United States for only a year and is still making progress in English) and whether other languages are in the process of being restructured, that is, being modified due to the influence of a stronger language. This would be the case, for example, with Hindi for a Hindi-French bilingual in France who has very little use of her Hindi because she has been living abroad for ten years.

The language history of the bilingual is a third thing to keep in mind. Which languages (and language skills) were acquired, and when? Were the languages acquired at the same time (something that is relatively rare) or one after the other? For example, many people acquire one language at home and then a second language when they start school. And how were the languages acquired? In a natural setting or more formally (at school), or a combination of both? How a language was acquired can have an impact on how well one knows it, especially regarding reading and writing competence. We also need to know what the pattern of language use was over the years. In sum, the age at which a language was acquired, how it was acquired, and the amount of use it has been given over the years has an impact on how well a language is known, how it is processed, and even the way the brain stores and deals with it. We will come back to this question in the chapter that deals with languages across the lifespan.

We also have to know about the bilingual's proficiency (fluency) in each of the four skills (speaking, listening, reading, writing) in each language. (So far we have mentioned only a global measure of fluency for each language.) A way of representing this, for a given moment in time, is to use four of the grids presented in Figure 2.1, one for each skill, filling in each one according to the use of the skill and the fluency in the skill. More complete proficiency tests can then be administered, as well as self-assessment questionnaires.[6] What one will find is that many bilinguals may not know how to read and write a particular language, even though they speak it and listen to it. In addition, their proficiency will rarely be equal across languages, as we discussed above, and they might have an accent in a language, a topic we will come back to in a later chapter.

Another important factor that characterizes bilinguals concerns the functions of their languages: which languages (and language skills) they use, in what context, for what purpose, and to what extent. We know, for example, that with many bilinguals only one language is used for certain specific domains (such as at work, for religious practices) whereas others may cross domains (as when several languages are used with friends). In the next chapter we will examine the influence this has on language dominance as well as on such behaviors as translation.

A full description of the bilingual also needs to take into account language mode, which is the state of activation of the bilingual's languages, depending on such factors as situation, interlocutor, and topic. In some situations, such as when speaking with monolinguals, only one language is active and being used. For instance, when I am addressing a French audience, only my French is present and I deactivate my other languages so that they do not intervene. In other situations, however, such as when speaking to another bilingual who shares the same languages, two or more languages can be active and can interact in the conversation. For example, when I speak French to my wife, who is bilingual in French and English, I may bring in words and sentences from English, depending on my need for them, as I know she will understand me. In this situation (called a bilingual mode), bilinguals can simply bring in the other language for a word, a phrase, or a sentence (through mechanisms called code-switching and borrowing), or they can actually change the language they are speaking (referred to as changing the base language). I will spend three full chapters on such phenomena, as they are central to bilingual communication.

A final factor to keep in mind is biculturalism: whether bilinguals interact with two or more cultures or whether they live their lives within one culture. Not all bilinguals are also bicultural. For example, a Moroccan who knows and uses Moroccan Arabic as well as Modern Standard Arabic and who has lived all his life in Morocco is bilingual but not bicultural. Nevertheless many bilinguals, such as first-generation immigrants, *are* also bicultural, and this plays a role in their bilingualism. We will discuss this in Chapter 10, "Bilinguals Who Are Also Bicultural."

3

The Functions of Languages

We will begin this chapter with a brief visit to the town of Pomerode, in the state of Santa Catarina in Brazil. In this community of some 20,000 inhabitants, founded by German immigrants from Pomerania in Germany, both German (more precisely, Pomeranian) and Portuguese are spoken by a majority of the population. What is interesting is how the inhabitants distribute their languages across the domains of their lives; some domains are covered by one language, some by the other, and some by both.[1] In certain situations, for example, only Portuguese is used (with the authorities, in clubs, for sports, for writing), in others only German is used (for example, at church), and in some areas both languages are employed (at work, in stores, at home, with friends).

What is true of Pomerode's Portuguese-Pomeranian bilinguals is true of most bilinguals throughout the world, whether they live in communities with other bilinguals or by themselves. They distribute their languages across the different domains of life and use different languages with different people. After a discussion of the principle describing this phenomenon, we will study the impact it has on bilinguals' language fluency, language dominance, and translation abilities, as well its less direct consequence for memory.

What Languages Are Used For

What I call the complementarity principle can be stated as follows:

Bilinguals usually acquire and use their languages for different purposes, in different domains of life, with different people. Different aspects of life often require different languages.

The complementarity principle is illustrated in Figure 3.1. In the figure, I have taken up our example of Ana from the previous chapter, and I have attributed her languages to the domains in which she uses them. To simplify things, I reduced the number of domains covered; in reality there would be many more. Ana's fourth language (Ld, French) is not represented in the figure as she never uses it. Each domain is represented by a hexagon and can be covered by one, two, or three languages. We see that La (English, Ana's best-known and most-used language according to the figure in Chapter 2) is used by itself in five domains of life: college, shopping, going out, boyfriend, and official matters. Language Lb (Spanish, also a highly used language but with medium fluency) is used by itself in two domains of life: with parents and with distant relatives; and La and Lb together cover three domains: siblings, friends, and religion. Finally, we note that Lc (Italian), which Ana does not use very much and does not know very well, shares just one domain with La and Lb (distant friend).[2]

For all bilinguals we can draw the same kind of language-use pattern covering domains such as parents, children, siblings, distant relatives, work, sports, religion, school, shopping, friends, going out, hobbies, and so on, and come up with a distribution of their languages. Some languages will cover many domains, others fewer, and some will cover domains along with another language

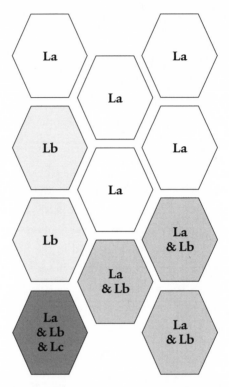

Figure 3.1. An illustration of the complementarity principle. The domains covered by languages La (English), Lb (Spanish), and Lc (Italian) are represented by the hexagons.

(or other languages). Rarely do bilinguals have all domains of life covered by all their languages (La *and* Lb at work, La *and* Lb at home, La *and* Lb with one's family). If all languages were used in all domains, there would probably be much less reason to be bilingual. Just one language would normally be sufficient.

It should be noted that with diglossia, a form of societal bilingualism where two languages or two varieties of a language are employed by a group, each language has a very precise domain of use. Thus the principle stated above is rigidified in diglossia: very few if any domains are covered by two or more languages.

The Impact of the Complementarity Principle

A first impact this principle has is on language fluency. In general, if a language is spoken in a reduced number of domains and with a limited number of people, then it will not be developed as much as a language used in more domains and with more people. It is precisely because the need for and uses of their languages are usually quite different that bilinguals do not develop equal and total fluency in all their languages. This is also true for certain language skills, such as reading and writing. Many bilinguals have not had to read and write in one or more of their languages and hence have not developed those skills. And even if they do have reading and writing skills in each language, the levels of competence are probably different because their need for those skills is not the same in everyday life.

If a domain is not covered by a language, bilinguals will simply not possess the domain-specific vocabulary, the stylistic variety, or even sometimes the discursive and pragmatic rules needed for that domain. Let me give a personal example. When I was on the faculty of Northeastern University in Boston in the 1970s and '80s, I taught introductory statistics, among other courses. I therefore knew the "language of statistics," but I knew it only in English. When I came back to Europe and offered to teach a statistics course in French, I suddenly found myself in difficulty. I simply didn't have the vocabulary in French and didn't know how to say such things as "standard distribution," "scattergram," "hypothesis test," and so on. It was a very odd feeling. My French is fluent and yet there I was, struggling to get concepts out.

I know that many bilinguals have shared the experience of suddenly having to use a language that they don't usually use in a particular domain. What happens then is interesting, but also frustrating at times. You tend to fumble in the language that is new in that domain. When you don't find the right word or expression, you are tempted to draw from the other language or languages you know, a tactic that sometimes works when you are speaking with other bilinguals who share your languages but that is inappropriate when you are speaking to monolinguals. So you continue to struggle and perhaps finally resort to bringing in some of the words from the other language(s) all the same, by adapting them and explaining them. Sometimes you simply try to shorten the conversation. As one bilingual writes:

> Whenever I have to explain in French anything about my professional activities or my former school experience in the U.S., I find it very hard not to use English words, because these experiences belong to my "English-related background." I have learned the business language in the U.S. and find it difficult to express the same ideas in French. Luckily this occurs most of the time with bilingual friends and therefore it doesn't bother anyone to switch from one language to another or to mix both in the same conversation.[3]

Three students of mine (Christine Gasser, Roxane Jaccard, and Vanessa Cividin) interviewed English-German and French-Italian bilinguals about domains that were linked to particular languages (such as work, family, shopping, hobbies).[4] Before the interviews, they learned how the subjects' languages were distributed across the domains, and they divided the domains into two categories for a particular language: a strong domain (a domain in which the language is used) and a weak domain (where the language is not used). They then observed how their subjects talked about these domains with them. (In the interviews, the subjects knew that they were speaking to fellow bilinguals and hence could call on their other language if they needed to.) What they found was that the subjects brought in their other language two to five times more often when they were speaking about a weak domain, as compared with a strong domain. In the weak domain they simply didn't have the vocabulary they needed to speak that language by itself and hence called upon the other, stronger language. This shows how hard it is to speak to someone in the "wrong" language—and things only get worse when that person is monolingual and does not know the speaker's more favorable language.

Well-learned behaviors are special cases for the complementarity principle, since one language has almost exclusive control of the behavior in question. For example, counting and mathematic computations are usually done in the language in which they were learned. An Arabic-English-French trilingual once wrote to me:

> There is one type of activity that I find I always use
> French for, and that is mental arithmetic. I learned arith-
> metic in French, and I find that I remember multiplica-
> tion tables best in that language and have continued us-
> ing it for that purpose.[5]

And an Alsatian-French bilingual stated:

> I do not know how to count in Alsatian very well. I have to think about numbers above twenty and especially about dates.[6]

I have known bilinguals who do simple arithmetic in one language and more advanced mathematics in another because they changed their language of instruction between the two. Praying is another specialized area where the complementarity principle is at work. Many bilinguals can recite a prayer in one language but have great difficulty doing so in another, simply because they did not learn it in that language. Phone numbers can also be a problem. When I lived in the United States I knew my phone number in English only, and I had to go through a painstaking process to convert it into French when I had to give it in that language (when speaking French with French-English bilinguals, I would simply switch to English for the phone number so as not to have to go through that process). Now that I am back in Europe, my current phone number is in French in my memory and its English version is simply much less available to me.

A second effect of the complementarity principle concerns language dominance. It is recognized in the field of bilingualism that many bilinguals are dominant in one of their languages, as opposed to being "balanced." Even though dominance is difficult to define (is it based on fluency only, on fluency and use, or on the ability to also read and write in the language?), most specialists put the emphasis on fluency: subjective fluency (as it is reported by the bilinguals themselves) and objective fluency (as it is evaluated by assessment tools).[7]

To assess subjective fluency, bilinguals are given language background questionnaires that include self-rating scales for their two or more languages and the four skills in each language (speaking, listening, reading, and writing).[8] Among the tools used for assessing objective fluency, one finds language evaluation measures taken by outside judges (including pronunciation evaluation) as well as behavioral tasks that measure, among other things, the time needed to do such things as carry out a command, name a picture or a number, read a text. These instruments also contain translation tasks. Based on the various measures obtained, evaluators determine a dominance rating: the person is dominant in Language a, or dominant in Language b, or balanced in both languages.

These various approaches have been criticized for reducing the complexity of the bilingual's language behavior to a number of rather simple tasks. Admittedly some assessments may produce a global measure of dominance—confirming, for example, that Ana (our example) is indeed globally dominant in La (English). In Figure 2.1, we saw that she is generally more fluent in La than in Lb (Spanish) and, of course, much more fluent in La than in Lc (Italian) or Ld (French). And in Figure 3.1 we observed that she covers many more domains with La than with Lb or Lc: nine in all for La, counting shared domains, as compared with six for Lb, and only one for Lc. So Ana does appear to be, at first sight, a "dominant" bilingual in English rather than a "balanced" bilingual. But the problem with global dominance assessments is that they do not take into account how the languages are distributed over domains. Even though Ana is globally dominant in La, we see that there are two domains in which she uses Lb exclusively. She is probably dominant in Lb in those domains, as could be shown with the right assessment tools. In fact, back in 1971 Robert Cooper had already shown evidence for this. He found that Spanish-English bilinguals had very different word-naming scores depending on whether the domain proposed was family, neighborhood, school, or religion. In some domains they would have been considered balanced, but not in others.[9] In sum, bilinguals should not be surprised that, even if they are globally dominant in a language, they may feel less dominant, or not dominant, in that language in a particular domain; this is simply a reflection of the complementarity principle at work.

A final effect of the principle concerns translation. Consider the following long-standing belief:

Myth: Bilinguals are born translators.

How often have we been asked as bilinguals, "Oh, since you're bilingual in X and Y, could you translate this for me?" And how often have we felt inadequate in proposing a translation? Of course we try to please our interlocutor (until the requests become too frequent or difficult), but we often have to explain why we couldn't do a very good job—because we didn't know several translation equivalents, for example, or didn't understand part of a domain-specific text. The response we get is invariably, "Oh, but I thought you were bilingual!"

Bilinguals' lack of translation skills can be explained by means of the complementarity principle. Unless bilinguals have domains covered with two languages, or they acquired the language they are translating into (the target language) in a manner that puts the emphasis on translation equivalents and thus on building a bridge between La and Lb, they may find themselves without the resources to produce a good translation. In given domains, they may be missing the required vocabulary and set expressions. This is exactly what happened to me when I had to translate statistical terms from English into French; I just didn't have them. In addition, bilinguals may lack stylistic variety in the target language, or the cultural or technical knowledge required to understand what is being said in the source language. Hence, even though bilinguals can usually translate simple things from one language to another, they often have difficulties with more specialized domains. This does not make them any less bilingual; it simply reflects the fact that their different languages are distributed across different domains of their lives and overlap only in some of them.

There is also a slightly less direct consequence of the complementarity principle that relates to memory. It seems that bilinguals remember things better when the language that is used for recall matches the language used at the time of the event in a particular domain. Researchers Viorica Marian and Ulrich Neisser mention two anecdotal pieces of evidence when introducing a study that confirms this point. The first anecdote was offered by the multilingual researcher Aneta Pavlenko. When asked, in Russian, for her apartment number in the United States, she erroneously provided the number of her old apartment in her native country, which she knew in Russian. The other anecdote was offered by Elizabeth Spelke, who related that a bilingual child had learned a French song while on vacation in France but could not recall the song on his return to the United States. However, when he was once again in a French-speaking environment, he remembered the song without any effort.[10]

For their study, Marian and Neisser interviewed a number of Russian-English bilinguals, in English and in Russian. They gave them English prompt words in the English part of the study, and Russian prompt words (translation equivalents) in the Russian part. The English prompt words included, for example, "summer," "neighbors," "birthday," "cat," "doctor." The task of the bilinguals was to describe an event from their own life that the prompt word brought to mind. The researchers also asked the participants, after the interview, to indicate the language in which they had been spoken to, they had spoken, or they had been surrounded by at the time that each recalled event took place. If the event prompted by the word "cat" took place in Russian, the researchers called this a Russian memory; if in English, then it was an English memory. They found that their bilingual subjects accessed more Russian memories when interviewed in Russian than when interviewed in English, and more English memories when interviewed in English than when interviewed in Russian. Marian and Neisser concluded that bilinguals are more likely to retrieve events (memories) that occurred in a particular language if that same language is also used in the retrieval setting. They called this language-dependent recall. Thus the complementarity principle also manifests itself in the recall of events that took place in the bilingual's different languages—which, as we have seen, are usually linked to different domains.

The complementarity principle is certainly one of the most pervasive aspects of individual bilingualism. Bilinguals who speak two or more languages feel its constant presence in their everyday lives. They may even comment openly on its different manifestations, without finding the exact words to account for them.

4

*Language Mode and
Language Choice*

When communicating with others, bilinguals have
to ask themselves two questions (which they often do subconsciously): which language should they use, and can they bring their
other language(s) into the interaction if they need to? Figure 4.1 illustrates the process of asking—and answering—these questions. To
simplify things, the example concerns someone who uses just two
languages; we will talk about tri- and quadrilinguals later.

The bilingual's two languages, which are visually represented by
the squares in the diagram, are inactive (or deactivated) before the
interaction (these squares are filled in with diagonal lines). In our
example, the bilingual answers the "which language" question with
Language a (La). It becomes activated and is then represented with
a solid black square. This first process, choosing which language to
use, is called language choice, and the language chosen is called the
base language.

The next question is whether the other language should be
brought in or not. If, for example, the bilingual is speaking to a
monolingual who does not know her other language, the answer is
no, and we see in the diagram (on the lower left) that the other lan-

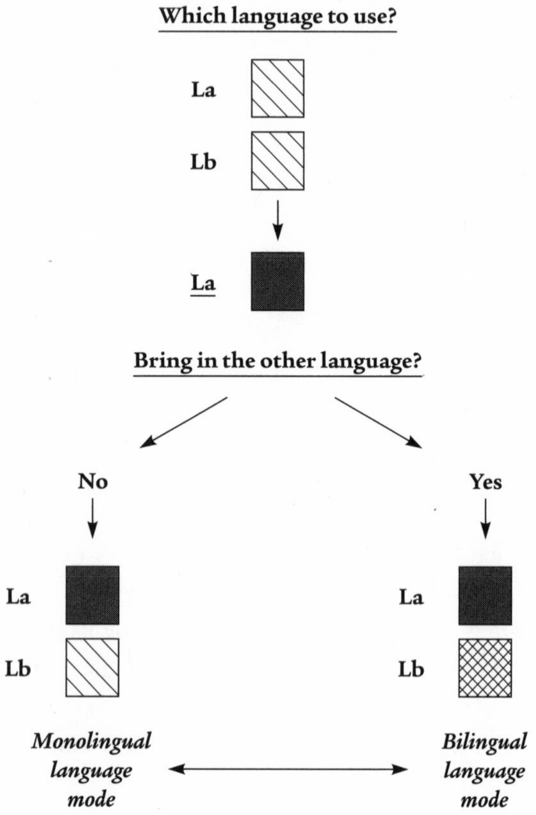

Which language to use?

La ▨

Lb ▨

↓

<u>La</u> ■

Bring in the other language?

No ↓

Yes ↓

La ■

Lb ▨

La ■

Lb ▧

*Monolingual
language
mode*

◀──────────▶

*Bilingual
language
mode*

Figure 4.1. Deciding which language to use and whether to bring in the other language.

guage (Lb) remains inactive; only La is active (solid black). In this situation, the bilingual is said to be in a monolingual language mode, as only one language is active. When my wife speaks to her aunt, for example, she chooses French as the base language and deactivates her English because she knows that her aunt would not understand her if she brought English into their conversation. She is, therefore, in a monolingual language mode. If, however, a bilingual is talking to another bilingual who shares her two languages (La and Lb), and she feels comfortable bringing in the other language with that person, then Lb will also be activated, but less so than La (see the cross-hatched lines filling the Lb square on the lower right). This situation is referred to as a bilingual language mode. Thus, when my wife and I talk to each other we choose French as our base language, but our English is also active and we sometimes bring it in to refer to places and people we know in Britain or the United States or to things we did in those places. With us, La is the most active language, as it is the base language, but Lb is on standby in case it is needed. Much of the bilingual's language behavior revolves around the possibilities offered in Figure 4.1, as we will see below and in the next two chapters.

Language Mode

Looking at Figure 4.1 again, we see that the monolingual language mode and the bilingual language mode are endpoints on a continuum (an arrow line links them). In their everyday lives, bilinguals find themselves at various points along this continuum that induce different language modes.[1] At one end of the continuum bilinguals are in a monolingual mode, as when they are speaking (or writing) to monolinguals in one of the languages they know (family members, friends, colleagues). They can also be in this mode if they are reading a book written in one of their languages, or watching a TV program in just one language. At the other end of the continuum, bilinguals find themselves in a bilingual language mode when they are communicating with bilinguals who share their two languages, such as close friends or siblings, and with whom they feel they can bring in the other language. They might also be in bilingual language mode when they are listening to a conversation between other bilinguals in which the two languages are used. Bilinguals can also be in an intermediary mode on the continuum, for example when their interlocutor is bilingual but does not like to bring in the other language during a conversation, or when they are talking about a subject in the "wrong" language (their other language is probably activated in such a situation, even if they do not use it).

Bilinguals differ from one another in terms of how much they move along the language-mode continuum. Some stay at the monolingual end, whereas others will move right along the continuum, choosing different points on it depending on the situation, the person they are speaking with, the topic, and so on. Those who live in bilingual communities may find themselves at the bilingual end of the continuum during the major part of their day. Movement along the continuum can occur at any time, as soon as there is a need for it. We might start at the monolingual end and then, halfway through a conversation, realize that the person we are talking to is also bilingual and move to the bilingual end. We might also start at the bilingual end and then come to understand, as the conversation takes place, that our interlocutor dislikes switching languages. We will then deactivate the other language and speak monolingually.

Many researchers believe that, in a monolingual mode, the language not being used is not totally deactivated (note that the squares in Figure 4.1 representing deactivated languages are not white but are partially filled in with diagonal lines). This is because bilinguals are often influenced by their other language, even in a monolingual situation. We can see this in the dynamic interferences they produce—that is, the deviations that are due to the deactivated language, such as when one says in English, "He liked very much the person" based on the French, "Il aimait beaucoup la personne."

In a bilingual mode, the base language is normally more active than the other ("guest") language, but there are instances when both need to be fully active, such as when a bilingual person is listening to two people speaking different languages or when he or she is interpreting. In the latter case, you need to have access to both the source language (the entering language) and the target language (the language you are interpreting into). Note also that in a bilingual mode the base language can change; one can start speaking La to an interlocutor and then change over to Lb by simply flip-flopping the levels of activation of the two languages (something that can't be done in the monolingual mode).

Then there is the case of the tri- or quadrilingual person. Figure 4.2 shows how a trilingual's languages can also be activated to different degrees. The trilingual has chosen Lb as the base language and has also activated Lc but not La, since the person she is speaking to knows just two of her three languages. She is therefore in a bilingual mode. With someone who knows the same three languages she does, and with whom she feels comfortable bringing in the other languages, she would be in a trilingual language mode. The same thing can happen with people who use four or more languages in their everyday life.

Choosing a Base Language

As we saw in Figure 4.1, bilinguals, when communicating in a bilingual mode, first have to choose a base language (also called a host

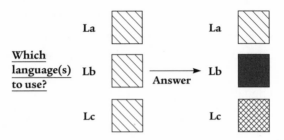

Figure 4.2. A trilingual in a bilingual mode.

or matrix language) to use with their interlocutors. The process of language choice is probably one of the most interesting bilingual phenomena, even though bilinguals don't give it much thought. Anthropologist Carroll Barber studied the language behavior of twelve trilingual Yaqui Indians of the Pascua Yaqui tribe in Arizona. She was interested in understanding when it was that they used Yaqui, Spanish, and English. She wrote:

> The men often find questions about their use of their
> languages rather ridiculous; naturally they speak Yaqui to
> Yaquis, Spanish to Mexicans, and English to Anglos. As
> one of them said, "I could talk to you in Yaqui—you
> wouldn't understand me." The problem does not seem so
> simple, however, when it is realized that in many of their
> social relationships they are dealing with people who
> speak at least two of their languages. Why then do they
> choose to speak one language at one time and another at
> some other time?[2]

Below, we will look at the factors for language choice according to four main categories: participants, situation, content of discourse, and function of the interaction. We will address the complexity of the phenomenon and see how it can sometimes break down.

Within the participants category, one factor that is crucial for language choice is the language proficiency of the speaker and the interlocutor. One usually attempts to use the language that will be the most successful for communication. I've heard many bilinguals state that they use language X with a certain person simply because she does not master the other language sufficiently well. Another factor that seems to play an important role is the language history between participants. One develops an "agreed upon" language with certain individuals, even if it has never been discussed, and this becomes the language of communication from then on. In fact, this agreement is so strong that an interlocutor may be puzzled or surprised if it is broken (for example, with a sudden change of base language over the phone).

A participant's attitude toward a language and a group may also explain language choice. Members of stigmatized minorities may no longer wish to speak the majority's language; this is true of people who have suffered in the past at the hands of the majority (such as German Jews during World War II and Russian Jews more recently, who refuse to use German and Russian, respectively, in their new countries). Other factors in the participants category include age, the socioeconomic status of the participants, their degree of intimacy, the power relationship between them, and so on.[3] What is fascinating here is that in bilingual communities, some bilinguals who deal extensively with the public, such as storekeepers, sales representatives, police officers, and others, develop a finely tuned sense for determining which language to use with a particular person. They base their decision on such cues as the person's stance, dress, and facial expression—and they are often right.

Concerning the next category, situation, the location of the interaction is an important language-choice factor. In bilingual Paraguay, for example, one will tend to address someone in the countryside in Guaraní but use Spanish in the cities.[4] Elsewhere, members of minorities may well speak the majority language when out in public together and keep their minority language for use when they are at home (I have noticed this with young North Africans in France). The formality of the situation is also important. In Switzerland, for example, Swiss German is not usually spoken by members of the federal government when they are giving a speech on TV (they will use German), although they will speak it as they are coming into the studio, and with friends and colleagues afterward. Of course, the presence of monolinguals is of crucial importance. How many times have I seen this situation: a group of people is speaking language X together until a monolingual of language Y arrives; they then switch over to language Y to include that person. But then the group switches right back to language X when the monolingual is having a side conversation or steps away for a few minutes! Unfortunately, a person can on occasion be left out because she does not master (or master sufficiently well) the language of the others. This can be quite frustrating, and usually something gives way quite rapidly—either the person wanders off or the others integrate her, even if it means having someone translate the major points of what is being said.

As for the content of discourse, we have already discussed this when dealing with the complementarity principle. Some topics are simply better dealt with in one language than another, and bilinguals speaking among themselves may well change base languages when they change topics. In Paraguay again, school, legal, and business affairs are usually discussed in Spanish rather than in Guaraní. I know I change languages, for example, when I talk about cognitive psychology with my son, with whom I normally speak French; we each have a larger vocabulary in English in that domain and it just simplifies things to move over to that language when we want to talk about some recent research.

Finally, concerning the fourth category, the function of the interaction, we should keep in mind that people often communicate to achieve something and not just to pass information along to someone else. Thus there are many instances of choosing a particular language to raise one's status, to create a social distance, to exclude someone, to request something, or to give a command. For example, Gerard Hoffman mentioned in his study that, in the Puerto Rican community in Jersey City, New Jersey, some Puerto Rican foremen would change languages when they changed roles: they would speak Spanish to the other Puerto Ricans at lunchtime but employ English during work hours, when their status changed to the role of foreman.[5] As for excluding someone, all bilinguals have "played" with language choice, although there is always the danger that it can backfire and create an embarrassing situation. I was once told by a young Greek American woman about a time when she was in a crowded student cafeteria with a friend with whom she normally spoke English. They changed over to Greek to comment on people around them, thinking they would not be understood. After a few minutes, one of the people they had talked about folded his newspaper, turned toward them, and said with a large grin, "Good-bye!" in Greek.

Usually several factors taken together explain a bilingual's language choice, and some factors have more weight than others. In her classic book on Guaraní-Spanish bilingualism in Paraguay, Joan Rubin states that three factors (countryside, school, and public functions in the capital city) clearly indicate which language to use (Guaraní for the first factor, Spanish for the other two) but that the rest can best be placed in a decision tree that orders them.[6] At the very top of the tree is location, then formality, then intimacy, then seriousness of discourse, and if you have not branched off before this point, there are still three remaining factors: the first language learned, the person's predicted proficiency, and the sex of the two participants. Not all language decisions require one to go through so many steps, but language choice remains complex even though it is a well-learned behavior that takes place smoothly and rapidly. Bilinguals are usually quite unaware of the many factors behind their choice; it is just part of being bilingual.

However hard one tries to find the right language for a given context, it may happen that a satisfactory solution cannot be found. I observed one such situation when my wife and I were sitting in a restaurant in the German part of Switzerland one day. I could not help but notice that the five people at the table right next to ours did not all share the same languages. I made a sketch of the situation at their table when I got back home (see Figure 4.3). Clearly the father, mother, and daughter in the group were visiting from the United States and had invited the daughter's grandmother and great-aunt to dinner. The father and daughter spoke the elders' languages (German and French) in addition to speaking the mother's only language (English). In the figure, I have indicated who communicated with whom and the language used (E for English, G for German, F for French). I also show, with the discontinuous lines, who could not communicate with whom: the mother with the grandmother and the mother with the great-aunt. Note that two people were pivotal throughout the meal, the father and the daughter. They knew and used all three languages and hence could ease the communication flow. This is a good example of the com-

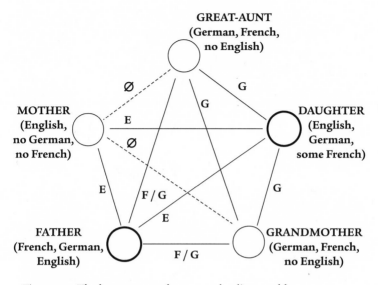

Figure 4.3. The languages spoken around a dinner table.

plexity one can find in language-choice situations, and also of the fact that some people may be marginalized when they do not share the others' language(s). It also shows how important go-betweens can be; they play a crucial role that can at times be quite taxing.

Another example reveals how a factor that at first sight should play the most important role in the choice of a base language may be put aside for a second, less important factor. I was sitting in my office one day when a student came in and asked in French, with great hesitancy and a very heavy American accent, whether I was Professor Grosjean. I replied that I was. Aware of my interlocutor's very poor French, and mindful of the importance of establishing good communication concerning an administrative matter, I suggested in English that we speak English. To my amazement, she did not take me up on my offer. She continued with her very hesitant French, which I had difficulty understanding. I asked again, in English, whether she did not wish to change over to English and was told, in French, that she had come to Switzerland to learn French and wanted to speak it. Hence, we continued in French, but since I wasn't sure we were understanding each other, I gave her some documents to take with her and wound down the interaction. Thinking back on it, I suppose I should have agreed to act as a language teacher and gone along with her wish to speak French, but it was a busy day and I didn't think we were communicating optimally. It made me grateful, though, that most interactions in language-choice situations are usually more smooth and efficient.

5

Code-Switching and Borrowing

We have seen that if a bilingual person is interacting with another bilingual who shares her languages, then a base language will be active during their communication and the other language will also be active, although less so. The bilingual speaker can bring in that other language if the need arises and if she feels comfortable doing so with her interlocutor. Here is an example. A French family is watching some ice fishermen on Walden Pond in the dead of the winter. The young son, Marc, shows real interest in the equipment being used and the fish that are brought up. The mother, who often brings in English when she is speaking French, is getting very cold and says to her husband: "Va chercher Marc *and bribe him* avec un chocolat chaud *with cream on top*." The French parts mean "go fetch Marc" and "with a hot chocolate," respectively. There are two ways of calling in the other, "guest" language: through what is called code-switching (as here) and through borrowing.

Code-Switching

Code-switching is the alternate use of two languages, that is, the speaker makes a complete shift to another language for a word, phrase, or sentence and then reverts back to the base language. Hence, bilinguals who code-switch are speaking language X in a bilingual mode when they call upon language Y for a moment. In the example above, the bilingual brings in whole phrases from English. Code-switching may also be done with single words, as in: "On a pris un *trail*" (We followed a trail), or whole clauses, as in the following Russian sentence with a code-switch into French: "Chustvovali, chto *le vin est tiré et qu'il faut le boire*" (They felt that the wine is uncorked and it should be drunk).[1]

Code-switching has often been criticized, mainly by monolinguals but also by some bilinguals. Many feel that it creates an unpleasant mixture of languages, produced by people who are careless in the way they speak. This has led to another common misconception:

Myth: Bilinguals code-switch out of pure laziness.

Code-switching has been given pejorative names such as Franglais (the mixture of English and French) and Tex-Mex (the combination of English and Spanish in the American Southwest). Reactions to code-switching can be rather strong. One is reported by Lynn Haney in her biography of the famous African American singer and dancer Josephine Baker. It should be recalled that Baker lived most of her adult life in France and spoke fluent French. Haney writes that when Baker returned to the United States on a visit, she was at a dinner party and was mixing some French into her English in addition to having sprinkles of French in her American accent. When she asked an African American maid for a cup of coffee, in French, the maid exclaimed that Baker was full of — and told her to speak the way her mouth was born![2]

Negative attitudes like these, as well as the worry that code-switching will lead to some form of "semilingualism," have led some bilinguals, such as language teachers and bilingual parents, to discourage code-switching and to avoid doing it. I would like to allay the reader's fears by quoting the distinguished linguist Einar Haugen, who wrote the following very sensible statement based on many years of research on bilinguals:

> Reports are sometimes heard of individuals who 'speak no language whatever' and confuse the two to such an extent that it is impossible to tell which language they speak. No such cases have occurred in the writer's experience, in spite of many years of listening to [their] speech.[3]

Personally, I have seen uncontrollable switching only in aphasic bilingual patients—that is, patients who have a language impairment stemming from a cerebral vascular accident (or stroke). But even then, it has been uncontrolled in just a handful of individuals; most aphasic patients control their code-switching well.

Bilinguals code-switch for many reasons. One primary reason is that certain notions or concepts are simply better expressed in the other language (they seek *le mot juste,* as one says in French). If the person you are speaking to understands your other language and accepts code-switches, and the better word or expression is from that language, then you can simply bring it into what you are saying. The analogy I use is having cream with coffee instead of just having it black; the word or expression in the other language adds a little something that is more precise than trying to find an equivalent element in the base language. The following is an example I have cited many times. My wife and I adopted the word "playground" as a code-switch when we were in the United States, as it reflected better the kind of free environment kids could have fun in, as compared with the traditional French *parc,* with its strict rules and rather poor offering of swing sets. (Since then, I'm happy to say, things have changed considerably in France and Switzerland and we, along with others, use a new expression that reflects this, *terrain de jeu.*)

A second reason for code-switching is to fill a linguistic need for a word or an expression. As we saw in Chapter 3 in the discussion of the complementarity principle, if a domain is covered wholly or partly by a language other than the one we are speaking, and the situation is conducive to code-switching, then we will bring in the words and expressions we need, either because they are the only ones we have or because they are the most readily available. As a French-English bilingual once wrote to me:

> The reason why I use so many words in English when I
> speak with French-speaking people is because I find it
> very hard to convey certain ideas or information about
> my daily life in this country [the U.S.] in a language other
> than English. Notions such as "day care center," "finger
> food," "window shopping," and "pot-luck dinners" need
> a few sentences to explain in French."[4]

For this bilingual woman, her home and young-children domains were covered mainly by English and so she code-switched into English when speaking about them. Another linguistic reason for code-switching is to report what someone has said in the other language. It would sound unnatural to translate it for a bilingual who understands the other language perfectly.

Code-switching is also used as a communicative or social strategy, to show speaker involvement, mark group identity, exclude someone, raise one's status, show expertise, and so on. As concerns exclusion, let me take an example from one of my earlier books. Nicole, a French-English bilingual in the United States, was a registered nurse in the cardiovascular unit of a large urban hospital on the East Coast. She spoke English at work, but since the arrival of a French Canadian colleague, she had sometimes been using French with her when they were alone. One day the two were asking a patient some questions about his recent heart attack. Toward the end of the interview, Nicole switched quickly into French without turning away from the patient and said softly: "Ça me paraît grave" (It seems serious). She then asked the patient a few more questions in English.[5] All bilinguals reading this can probably think of one or two times in their own experience when they rapidly slipped into another language to convey something to just one of the people they were with. But this can be a risky communicative strategy, in addition to being perceived as impolite, as the person being excluded may know the other language well enough to understand what has just been said.

An example of code-switching used to raise one's status was given by linguist Carol Myers-Scotton and her coauthor William Ury. The scene takes place on a bus in Nairobi. A passenger gets on and the conductor tells him, in Swahili, that the fare is fifty cents to go to the post office. The passenger gives him a shilling and the conductor tells him to wait for his change. When the bus nears the post office and the change still hasn't been handed over, the passenger tells the conductor that he wants his change. The conductor replies that he'll get his change. The passenger then switches over to English and says, "I am nearing my destination." The switch is an attempt by the passenger to change his status from equal to higher than the driver and hence to have more authority (English is the language of the educated elite in Kenya). But in this case, the conductor counters the attempt by saying, in English, "Do you think I could run away with your change?" thereby reestablishing status equality between them.[6]

It is interesting to note that code-switching can also take place in different modalities. Some bilinguals code-switch when writing, for example (in letters, e-mail messages, and so on) but they have a tendency to flag the words with quotation marks or by means of underlining. They are aware that the reader might be led astray if this precaution is not taken. Of course when you are writing for yourself (for example, taking notes) anything goes, and many of us bilinguals take multilingual notes full of unflagged switches. Code-switching can also take place between an oral language and a sign language. Paul Preston, himself an English–American Sign Language bilingual, interviewed a number of bilingual hearing adults, the children of Deaf parents. While most of the interviews took place in English, he noticed that his informants would sometimes switch to sign language. The reasons he gives are very similar to the ones we have already mentioned: his informants code-switched when they felt that a sign expressed a concept better, when they were momentarily unable to think of the English word, when they were paraphrasing Deaf people, and when they became emotionally unable to speak.[7]

In recent years, considerable work has been done by linguists to better understand how code-switching takes place.[8] One of the results has been the realization that, instead of being a haphazard and ungrammatical mixture of two languages, code-switching follows very strict constraints and is implemented by bilinguals who are competent in their languages. Linguist Shana Poplack, a pioneering expert on code-switching, writes:

> Code-switching is a verbal skill requiring a large degree of
> linguistic competence in more than one language, rather
> than a defect arising from insufficient knowledge of one
> or the other . . . [R]ather than representing deviant be-
> havior, [it] is actually a suggestive indicator of degree of
> bilingual competence.[9]

My own work on the phonetics of code-switching shows that there is indeed a sudden and complete sound shift to the other language at the switch break but that the prosody may, at times, remain that of the base language.[10] In a pilot study I conducted with my colleague Carlos Soares, we showed that if a code-switch is short and corresponds to a minor syntactic unit, as in the example at the beginning of this chapter, then it is integrated into the prosody of the base language. If, on the contrary, it is longer and a more important syntactic unit, then it will bring with it the prosodic patterns of the guest language. Thus, in the sentence, "Marc, savonne-toi. *You haven't used soap for a week!*" the first part, which can be translated as "Marc, soap yourself," has the characteristics of French prosody (a long falling contour) whereas the second part maintains its typical English prosodic pattern (a final rise indicating surprise). As for the listener's perception of a code-switch, how efficient it is will depend on such factors as the specificity of sounds and groups of sounds in the guest language (the more specific, the easier the perception), the existence of a similar-sounding word in the base language (this has a tendency to delay the perception), the number and frequency of code-switches, and so on.

Borrowing

Another way bilinguals bring in their less activated language is by borrowing a word or short expression from that language and adapting it morphologically (and often phonologically) into the base language. Unlike code-switching, which is the alternate use of two languages, borrowing is the integration of one language into another. Figure 5.1 illustrates this.

As we can see in the top part of the figure, which depicts a code-switch, the person speaking Language a (La; empty rectangles) shifts over completely to Language b (Lb; shaded rectangle) and then switches back to La (empty rectangles again). With borrowing, on the other hand, the element borrowed from Lb is integrated into La; this is shown in the bottom part of the figure by the rectangle with diagonal lines, depicting the "blending" of Lb and La.

There are two forms of borrowing. Probably the most frequent is when both the form and the content of a word are borrowed (to

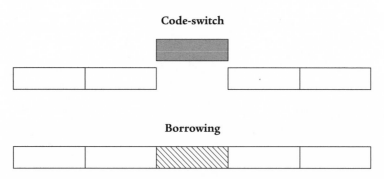

Figure 5.1. Illustration of the difference between a code-switch (the alternate use of two languages) and a borrowing (the integration of one language into the other).

produce what has been called a loanword or nonce borrowing, or more simply a borrowing), as in these two examples taken from French-English bilinguals: "Ça m'étonnerait qu'on ait *code-switché* autant que ça" (I can't believe we code-switched as often as that) and "Maman, tu peux me *tier* /taie/ mes chaussures?" (Mummy, can you tie my shoes?). In these examples, the English words "code-switch" and "tie" have been brought in and integrated into the French sentence. The parts of speech that are borrowed the most are nouns, followed by verbs (as in the above examples) and adjectives; the other parts of speech are borrowed much less often.

The integration of borrowings has been the object of much research. There is still some controversy surrounding their phonological adaptation (are they fully adapted to the base language or do they keep some of their guest-language phonology?) but there is less debate about morphological adaptation. As we can see in the examples above, the English word "code-switch" is brought into French and given the past-participle "-é" ending; the same is true in the second example, where the infinitive "-er" ending (pronounced /e/) is given to the English word "tie." When nouns are concerned, they are adapted to the noun morphology of the base language—for example, they may be given a plural form and a gender when the borrowing language requires it. Thus we find the following English borrowings in Spanish: "el *trainer*," "esa *girl*" (this girl), and "la *responsibility*."[11] Note that when a borrowing comes into a sentence and does not require a morphological marking, and if is not phonologically integrated—that is, pronounced with the phonetics of the base language—it is difficult to distinguish it from a one-word code-switch. This has caused much debate among specialists about whether we are dealing with a code-switch or a borrowing.

A second type of borrowing, called a loanshift, occurs when the speaker either takes a word in the base language and extends its meaning to correspond to that of a word in the other language, or rearranges words in the base language along a pattern provided by the other language and thus creates a new meaning. An example of the first kind of loanshift would be the use of *humoroso* by Portuguese Americans to mean "humorous" when its original meaning in Portuguese is "capricious." Another example would be *soportar* in Puerto-Rican Spanish; it normally means "to endure" but has now also been given the English meaning "to support." As for the rearranging of words, also called calques or loan translations, an example was noted in Florida in the Spanish speech of bilinguals who said *tener buen tiempo* (based on the English "to have a good time") instead of using the Spanish *divertirse*.[12] Another example of this kind would be: "I put myself to think about it," said by a Spanish-English bilingual, based on the Spanish expression *me puse a pensarlo*.[13]

Why do bilinguals borrow? The reasons are very similar to the ones given for code-switching, although there are fewer communicative strategies in play. Using the right word is at the top of the list, along with using a word from a domain covered by the other language (yet one more example of the complementarity principle at work). Linguists have spent considerable time explaining why immigrants, when speaking their native tongue, borrow so much from their host country's language. Practically overnight, they find themselves living with new realities and new distinctions in domains such as work, housing, schooling, food, sports, flora and fauna, and so on. Very often the vocabulary of their first language is not adequate to cover this new life. As Uriel Weinreich, the well-known researcher on bilingualism, once said, it is only natural to use ready-made designations from the other language instead of coining new words; after all, few users of language are poets![14]

It is important to distinguish the spontaneous borrowings of bilinguals (also called speech or nonce borrowings) from words that have become part of a language community's vocabulary and that monolinguals also use (called language borrowings or established loans). The latter, while originally brought in by bilinguals, are now used by all speakers of the language. In the following sentences, every third or fourth word is an established loan from French that has now become part of the English language: The _poet_ lived in the _duke's_ manor. That day, he _painted,_ played _music,_ and wrote _poems_ with his _companions_. The process through which some borrowings used by bilinguals become integrated into the monolingual's language is complex and has a number of variants: some words are borrowed very quickly while others go through a long process; some are brought in by one bilingual and others are accepted by a large bilingual community before being transferred to the monolingual group. Weinreich likens spontaneous borrowings to sand being carried by a stream, whereas established borrowings are like the sand that is deposited at the bottom of a lake.[15] Whether the sand keeps moving or is deposited depends on many factors; the same is true of borrowings.

When spontaneous borrowings become established borrowings, they have not only gone through an integration process but have also survived the resistance of some of the speakers of the language concerned. One may think of the French as being opposed to using English words, but some segments of the population do not hesitate— often unconsciously—to replace older, worn-out French words or expressions with new ones from English. Hence the existence of new English words in today's French, such as "cool," "top," "look," "best of," "too much," and the like. Having said this, there are institutions that attempt to reduce the amount of borrowing that takes place. In France, for example, the French Academy regularly proposes French words to replace English words for new concepts. Some are adopted by the French (*courriel* is now used as frequently as "e-mail") but others are simply not used, such as *bouteur* instead of "bulldozer." Languages know how to make good use of new words, and words can take on a life of their own. Take an example from French: the word "people" has now been borrowed into French, but with the meaning of celebrities (movie or soap stars, singers, actors). It has been fully integrated into the language and is now sometimes written as *les pipols*. This has led to such derivatives as *la pipolisation*.

The opposition to loans from other languages is not something new, and it has not always worked in the same direction. Back in 1300, Robert of Gloucester wrote the following about the domination of French over English:

> If a man knows no French, people will think little of him
> . . . I imagine there are in all the world no countries that
> do not keep their own language except England alone.[16]

Who could have thought that seven hundred years later the situation would be reversed, with English influencing French.

6

Speaking and Writing Monolingually

When communicating with others, bilinguals are constantly asking themselves—subconsciously most of the time—which language they should use and whether they can bring in another language. When they are in a monolingual language mode—that is, in the presence of monolinguals, or bilinguals who do not share their languages (or with whom they don't feel they can code-switch or borrow)—the answer is apparently quite simple: they will have to use the language the others know, and, if possible, they will not let another language intervene. But things are not always straightforward concerning the second point, the presence of the other, nonactive language.

Choosing a Language

At first sight, choosing a language for communicating in a monolingual mode appears to be a simple operation. We "shut off" our other language or languages and speak just one. After all, if we were to start speaking a language that our interlocutors did not know, we wouldn't get very far. As the Yaqui Indian mentioned earlier said, "I could talk to you in Yaqui—you wouldn't understand me."[1] I have been impressed over the years by how bilinguals excel at choosing the appropriate language and how proficient they are in deactivating their other languages. Suddenly, bi- or multilinguals who have two or more languages at their disposal can become speakers of a single language. I often think of tennis champion Roger Federer, who gives interviews in four languages (Swiss German, German, English, and French) and usually does so without letting his other languages intervene. In such situations, he is most often in a monolingual mode, as he can't expect that the interviewers, and especially the public he is speaking to, will know his other languages.

Bilinguals who manage to stay in a monolingual mode and, in addition, who speak that language fluently and have no accent in it, can often "pass" as monolinguals. I was quite surprised one day, several years ago, when I heard the baker's wife down the road from where I live answer the phone in fluent Swiss German. I had known her for some ten years and had always believed that she was Swiss French. I would have expected that she would have to struggle with German like most Swiss French do (not to mention with Swiss German, which the Swiss French rarely speak). But she was conducting a fluent conversation in what, I was to find out, was her mother tongue. I was just as surprised when I learned that the actress Natalie Wood, who starred in the 1961 movie *West Side Story,* and whom I had thought of as a totally monolingual person, was in fact born into a Russian-speaking family and was bilingual in Russian and English. Many examples come to mind of this "miracle" of bilingualism—the hidden languages that people know but have never used in our presence.

Choosing a base language and sticking to it for monolingual

communication, whether when speaking or writing, is just part of being a bilingual. Sometimes more than communication is at stake, and keeping to the monolingual mode is all the more crucial. Olivier Todd, the Franco-English journalist and writer, describes in his autobiography how his British mother and he had missed the last boat to England when the Germans invaded France. They remained in France for the duration of the war and his mother was in partial hiding, as she would have been sent to an internment camp if the Germans had known her nationality. Todd explains how they had agreed not to speak English in public—on the street, in cafés, on the bus. If an English word or sentence ever escaped her, Todd, who was a child at the time, was to squeeze her hand. The problem was that his mother was very anti-German, and one day on the Métro she burst out against the occupiers in English, right in front of a German officer. Todd tells us that they were lucky that day and nothing happened. Olivier Todd's mother made it through the war without being identified as a British subject.[2]

Researchers have long been intrigued by how bilinguals manage to control the language they speak and how they keep out their other languages. On a cognitive level there is active debate about the mechanisms involved. Some researchers, such as David Green of the University of London, talk of the inhibition of the languages not needed, whereas I take a "softer" stance and advocate the deactivation of those languages but not their inhibition.[3] I believe that the bilingual language system has to allow for switching back and forth between a monolingual and a bilingual mode, and that even in a monolingual mode, as we will see below, the speaker can call upon the other deactivated language. This is more difficult to do when a language is inhibited than when it is deactivated.

Neurologists and neurolinguists have recently conducted brain-imaging studies in an effort to better understand the structures that control language choice. Jubin Abutalebi and David Green reviewed the literature, and they suggest that several neural structures of control play a role: the left caudate in the subcortical area of the brain appears to supervise the correct selection of languages; the left prefrontal cortex updates and keeps on line the relevant language, as well as inhibits the languages not being used; the anterior cingulate cortex signals to the prefrontal cortex potential errors in language choice; and the left and right posterior parietal cortex biases selection toward the language in use and away from the language not in use.[4] This research, which is still very recent, is helping us understand how bilinguals select the right language to use and keep out the others, to some extent at least, as we will see below.

When bilinguals are in a monolingual mode, that is, speaking or writing in just one language, we expect that their other languages are deactivated and do not intervene. This would make sense, since the bilinguals are usually communicating with people who do not know the other languages. In fact, however, things are not quite as simple as that. Bilinguals may sometimes code-switch when speaking or writing monolingually, and they regularly produce interferences. We will examine both processes below.

Code-Switching in a Monolingual Mode

One reason for code-switching in a monolingual mode is to bring in a proper noun from the other language. Some bilinguals prefer to pronounce names (of a city, a newspaper, a person, even one's own name) in their correct language, which may force them to code-switch, whereas other bilinguals will adapt them phonologically into the base language, thus borrowing them in. There are no rules here. On the one hand, we don't want to sound too sophisticated or distant by switching over to the other language. It is also important that our interlocutors understand us, and code-switching might cause miscomprehension. On the other hand, adapting a name into the base language might distort it too much or detach it from reality. After all, an American friend named Jonathan just doesn't seem to be the same person when his name is pronounced in French. Deciding whether to say the proper noun in its original form or adapt it to the language being spoken will depend on many factors, but the central factors are clear communication and not distancing oneself too much from interlocutors. When I lived in the United States, I would anglicize my family name and then spell it out; giving the French version was not a solution, as most people simply wouldn't understand it.

Proper nouns aside, bilinguals may well code-switch momentarily when in a monolingual mode, either because they have not mastered the language that well (as when a highly dominant bilingual is speaking in his weaker language) or they do not have the required vocabulary for that particular domain in the language they are speaking (the complementarity principle). When they code-switch out of the blue like this, their interlocutors will often be taken aback. I've had people spring a code-switch on me when I didn't expect it and have been momentarily "deaf" to it. This simply shows how deactivated the other language can be when one is in a monolingual mode.

When the interlocutor, or one of the interlocutors, knows the speaker's other language, he or she can propose the translation equivalent in the language that is being spoken. This is a common strategy in multilingual countries, where people often understand several languages even if they prefer not to speak them, and they are ready to help out a bit. I once heard an American professor say on a French radio program during an interview, "Il n'est pas *ruthless*" (He's not ruthless). The reporter, who wanted the interview to be understandable to the listeners, came in immediately with the French expression, "sans scrupules." The professor said, "Oui . . ." and then continued what he had been saying.

If the interlocutor does not seem to know the bilingual speaker's other languages, then a code-switch will need to be accompanied by an explanation. One produces the word or expression in the other (guest) language, perhaps with a preceding phrase such as, "In language X we say . . . ," and then one proceeds. Of course, this cannot be done too often, because it slows down the interaction and may not be looked upon favorably by those listening.

Interferences

Despite the fact that bilinguals sometimes want to keep out their other languages when they are speaking or writing monolingually, and although they may have filtered out all code-switches, the other languages can still enter in the form of interferences: deviations from the language being spoken (or written) stemming from the influence of the deactivated languages. Interferences, also called transfers, accompany bilinguals throughout their life, however hard they try to avoid them. They are the bilingual's uninvited "hidden companions," often present even though one tries to filter them out.

Interferences are of two kinds: static interferences, which reflect permanent traces of one language on the other (such as a permanent accent, the meaning extensions of particular words, specific syntactic structures, and so on), and dynamic interferences, which are ephemeral intrusions of the other language, as in the case of an accidental slip on the stress pattern of a word due to the stress rules of the other language, or the momentary use of a syntactic structure taken from the language, or languages, not being spoken. In what follows, I will not distinguish between the two types of interference. Usually they are difficult to separate—except in the case of an accent, which is most often a static interference.[5] The discussion will emphasize dynamic interferences—elements of the other language that slip into the language you are speaking or writing, most often without your being aware of them. It is only when your interlocutor asks what you meant by word X or corrects your syntax or looks at you in a strange way that you realize, after the fact, that the other language has slipped in. You are often left with the feeling that you were *sure* that X was a word in that language, or that the structure was correct, when in fact that was not the case. (I was interested to see the interferences the copy editor of this book found after I sent the manuscript to the publisher; there were a few, even though I was working in a monolingual mode and trying to write in English only—except for examples, of course.)

It is important at this stage to differentiate interferences from other deviations that are due to the level of fluency attained in a language. These intralanguage deviations reflect the person's interlanguage (the linguistic knowledge level reached in the language) and may include overgeneralizations (for example, taking irregular verbs and treating them as if they were regular) and simplifications (dropping pluralization and tense markers, omitting function words, simplifying the syntax), as well as hypercorrections and the avoidance of certain words and expressions.

Interferences can occur at all levels of language. At the first level, that of pronunciation (phonology, prosody), a "foreign accent" is a direct reflection of the interference of another language. Traces of an accent can be permanent (it is simply the accent you have when you are speaking language X) or ephemeral, such as momentary slips in the pronunciation of a sound, the wrong stress placement on a word, the intonation of a phrase based on your stronger language, and so on. These accidental slips, which often increase in number when you are tired or stressed, will often "give you away" as a speaker of the other language. Your interlocutor may then ask you what other language you speak, or may—very nicely—tell you how well you speak the language you are using.

Interferences at the word level (individual words or expressions) resemble the lexical borrowings that we examined in the preceding chapter. In fact they may well be explained by similar psycholinguistic mechanisms, although this has not been studied adequately. Just like borrowings, you can import, involuntarily of course, both the form and the meaning of a word. Thus, a French-English bilingual once said to her English-speaking nephew, "Marc, you're *baving!*" She pronounced "baving," based on the French word *baver* (to dribble), like "patting." Marc looked at his aunt with puzzlement and she quickly corrected herself. Another example would be, "Look at the *camion!*" where the French word *camion* (truck) is pronounced as if it were an English word (like "canyon").

A more subtle type of lexical interference—the bête noire, so to speak, of bilinguals—is similar to a loanshift, where only the meaning of the word is brought in and added to an existing word. For example, in the sentence, "Look at the *corns* on that animal," the meaning of French *cornes* (horns) has been added to that of the English word "corn." Another example would be, "Oh, he's in the *stove,*" which a Norwegian American boy said when a stranger asked him where his father was. The interference comes from the Norwegian *stova,* which means living room.[6] In these two examples, the base- and guest-language words resemble each other to a large extent (they are near homophones, and near homographs when written; often called "false friends"), but that does not have to be the case, as we see in the example "Don't move the *needles* on the clock," based on the French word *aiguilles* (which means both needles and hands of a clock); the word should have been "hands." These accidental borrowings (loanshifts) can occur frequently in a bilingual's language because the words pronounced are definitely those of the base language and the bilingual believes he or she is speaking just one language, and yet the words are used with the wrong meaning. Nancy Huston, the Canadian and French bilingual writer, reports that she ends up avoiding the use of false friends such as *éventuellement* and "eventually," "harassed" and *harassé,* to make sure that she won't mix them up.[7]

Interferences at the level of idiomatic expressions and proverbs are also very frequent and particularly difficult to filter out. Bilinguals may translate them literally from the other language into the language they are speaking and not be aware that the meaning is not always transparent. Hence, "I'm telling myself stories" is a literal English translation of the French expression "je me raconte des histoires"; the bilingual speaker should have said, "I'm kidding myself."[8] Another example would be the literal translation of "as alike as two peas in a pod," which would not mean anything in French; one should say "comme deux gouttes d'eau" (literally, "like two drops of water"). Here are two examples where the literal English translation of a German expression comes close but isn't quite right: "Winter is before the door" is based on "Winter steht vor der Tür"; the English expression is "Winter is around the corner." And

"He was laughing in his fist" comes from "Er hat sich ins Fäustchen gelacht"; the correct English expression is "He was laughing up his sleeve."[9]

Interferences at the level of syntax are also quite frequent, such as when bilingual speakers use the word-order pattern of one language in the other, insert determiners when they are not normally present, use the wrong preposition (again based on the deactivated language), and so on. For example, if French-English bilinguals say "on *the* page five" instead of "on page five," they are probably thinking of the French equivalent, "sur la page cinq." The same is true of "I saw that *at* the television," based on "J'ai vu ça à la télévision."

As for interferences when writing, many are similar to the ones that crop up in spoken language at different linguistic levels (for example, lexical and syntactic). Among the things that are specific to writing, though, one finds spelling differences between languages. For instance, near homographs—that is, words that are spelled only slightly differently in two languages—are often a problem. Many English-French bilinguals have to stop and think about how many *d*'s there are in "address" (there is only one in French), how many *p*'s in "development" (there are two in French), if there are two *h*'s or not in "rhythm" (there is only one in French), and so on. Personally, I bless the development of grammar and spelling checkers in word processing programs, especially for difficult languages like French that have complex grammatical rules. However, word processors do not catch errors in higher-level aspects of language use, such as style and level of formality. These can be quite different in two languages (for example, the greeting and farewell phrases in letters, the style of reports, and so on) and we can easily write something incorrectly based on what we know from another language.

Interferences and Communication

The interferences bilinguals produce when communicating in a single language can have different impacts on the comprehension of their monolingual listeners (or readers). At the level of sentence structure, Uriel Weinreich proposed three categories, which we will address in order of the least impact to the greatest impact. In the first category, the interference pattern is possible in the base language and has no negative impact on comprehension. Thus an English-Russian bilingual who uses a subject-verb-object order in Russian, based on the normal English word order, produces a perfectly good Russian sentence, although that particular word order is not a necessity in Russian. In the second category of interferences, the meaning of the sentence is understandable by implication. Weinreich cites the German-English bilingual who says "yesterday came he," based on the German, "gestern kam er." Although the English sentence is not grammatical, the meaning can be understood. Finally, in the third category, the interference produces an unintended meaning and hence communication is affected.[10] I like to cite an example that caused me problems in my teenage years as a bilingual. I would say to French friends, "Je te manque," based on "I miss you" in English. My friends would look at me with a puzzled expression because I was in fact telling them that *they* were missing *me* instead of that I was missing them. I should have said, "Tu me manques."

Since instances of Weinreich's first two categories of interference seem to occur much more frequently, interferences seldom affect communication. In the long term, bilinguals who need to communicate in a particular language, either by speaking or writing, or both, will normally develop enough skills in the language to communicate satisfactorily. The interferences they produce will likely not be that numerous. In addition, monolinguals who live or work with bilinguals grow accustomed to language that is influenced by the other tongue. They get used to hearing an accent, strange sentence structures, words that are not quite appropriate, and this makes communication easier. An interesting example comes from English-American Sign Language (ASL) bilinguals, who sometimes retain facial expressions from sign language when communicating in an English monolingual mode. Paul Preston mentions the occasional use of prolonged eye contact, which is crucial in Deaf culture but which makes hearing people uncomfortable. In addition, he evokes the arched, furrowed eyebrows that are part of asking a "what, where, who, which" type of question in ASL, a facial expression that can be misunderstood as accusatory or angry in the hearing world.[11]

Many bilinguals have reported making more errors (many of them being interferences) when they are tired or stressed. Sentence structures that are normally controlled, morphological endings that are normally inserted, intonations that are usually mastered— all of these things can start breaking down in certain conditions. Nancy Huston evokes this with humor:

> The use of a foreign tongue discourages not only loquacity but pedantry; it prevents you from taking yourself too seriously . . . The minute I start yelling at my children, for instance, my accent worsens and my vocabulary shrinks— this makes them burst out laughing and I can no longer make my rage credible; I have no choice but to calm down and laugh.[12]

A final point concerns the direction of interferences. If bilinguals are heavily dominant in a language, then the interference flow is straightforward: the stronger language influences the weaker language, either in a permanent manner (perhaps in the form of an accent) or in an ephemeral way (what we have called dynamic interferences). However, if the two languages have more or less equal importance (at least in everyday use), then interferences can go both ways. The British researcher Vivian Cook is well known for his work showing how knowledge and use of a second language can have an influence on the first language.[13] When interferences are bidirectional, some bilinguals may report that they know neither language well, or that their languages are influencing each other. Eva Hoffman, in *Lost in Translation,* states this very appropriately:

> When I speak Polish now, it is infiltrated, permeated, and
> inflected by the English in my head. Each language
> modifies the other, crossbreeds with it, fertilizes it. Each
> language makes the other relative. Like everybody, I am
> the sum of my languages.[14]

In various writings, I have insisted on what I call the bilingual or holistic view of bilingualism, which proposes that the bilingual is an integrated whole who cannot easily be decomposed into two separate parts.[15] The bilingual is not the sum of two (or more) complete or incomplete monolinguals; rather, he or she has a unique and specific linguistic configuration. The coexistence and constant interaction of the languages in the bilingual have produced a different but complete language system.[16] The analogy I use is that of the high hurdler in track and field who blends two competencies, that of the high jumper and that of the sprinter, but is neither one alone.

In sum, the influences of the other language, notably in the form of interferences, are present in bilingual language but they do not usually affect communication. I would even suggest that they may render what is said more original and less stereotypical. As we will see, the prose of such bilingual writers as Joseph Conrad and Samuel Beckett contains traces of their other language. Interferences greatly enriched their writing and helped make it what it is.

7

Having an Accent in a Language

Even though very few of us are professional linguists, we all have something to say about a person's accent. An accent is one of the things that we notice most in someone's speech and we always have an opinion about it. The issue of accents gets more complicated with bilinguals and their two or more languages, especially because of a popular belief:

Myth: Real bilinguals have no accent in their different languages.

The reality for bilinguals is quite different. Having a "foreign" accent in one or more languages is, in fact, the norm for bilinguals; not having one is the exception. Whether one has an accent mainly depends on when the language was acquired. Having an accent does not make someone less or more bilingual. Some extremely fluent and balanced bilinguals have an accent in one or the other of their languages; other less fluent bilinguals may have no accent at all. The world is full of respected scholars, writers, politicians, and others who are bilingual and speak with an accent in one of their languages.

Take, for example, the illustrious author Joseph Conrad, mentioned briefly at the end of the preceding chapter. What one tends to forget about Conrad is that he was originally Polish, not British, and that he had a very strong Polish accent when he spoke in English. And yet his English prose is recognized as outstanding and he remains one of English literature's great authors of the turn of the twentieth century. In a totally different domain, a recognized American statesman and Nobel Prize winner, Henry Kissinger, has a strong German accent when speaking in English, a language that he masters fully.

In sum, there is no relationship between one's knowledge of a language and whether one has an accent in it. Because accents are in fact normal among bilinguals, we will examine why people have accents, what they mean at the phonetic level, and the disadvantages and advantages for bilinguals of having an accent.

An Accent: Why and How

One can have an accent in a language for several reasons. First, and quite simply, it can be because one has acquired a particular dialect of the language. Thus an English speaker from India may simply have the accent linked to Indian English and it may have nothing to do with the age at which his English was acquired. A second, better-recognized reason is the influence of one's first language on the second. An English-French bilingual may have an English accent in French because she acquired French later on in life. This was the case for my English great-aunt, who had moved to France in her twenties. She had a strong accent when she spoke French, although her French was otherwise impeccable and quite refined.

What kind of influence can the first (often stronger) language have on the second (often weaker) language? First, if the latter has a sound that isn't found in the first, the speaker may use a replacement that is phonetically close. For example, because there is no "z" sound in Norwegian, Norwegians speaking English sometimes say "rosses" instead of "roses." There is no "ch" sound in Portuguese (as in "church") and so a Portuguese person speaking English may say "shicken" instead of "chicken." The same is true for the English "th" sound replaced by "s" or "z" or "f" or "v" by French speakers, who may say "sanks" instead of "thanks." Note also that if the second (or weaker) language has two rather similar sounds where the first (stronger) language has only one, the bilingual may fail to distinguish the two sounds and use only one, based in part on the first language. Thus, a French person may use the same sound when pronouncing "hit" and "heat," "rim" and "ream," and so on. At the level of prosody, word stress can be particularly difficult to master. Instead of stressing the first syllable in "LI-brary," a French person may say, "LI-BRA-RY." This pronunciation is still understandable to an English-speaking listener, but when the stress is put on the wrong syllable (and the others are reduced), intelligibility problems can occur, for example, with "e-DIN-burgh" instead of "E-dinburgh."

An accent can also be caused by the second language's influence on the first. This can happen after many years of greater use of the second language and reduced use of the first. I once met a French woman who had learned English when she came over to the United States with her husband, whom she had met on a U.S. military base in France. She had lived in the Midwest, far removed from any French speakers, and she had rarely returned to France. When I met her, some twenty years later, she spoke French with a rather strong American English accent: her intonation in French was English, her stop consonants ("p," "t," "k") were aspirated and no longer French, and so on. She was very conscious of the change and I spent the greater part of our conversation telling her it was quite natural that she would have an accent in French, given the circumstances of her life.

What about an accent in a third or a fourth language: where does it come from? It really depends on when and where one has acquired the language. For example, I acquired my Italian in my teens when English was my stronger language (although it's not my first language), and so I have an English accent in Italian. Had I acquired it earlier, I might have a French accent in Italian or no accent at all. One should also note that a bilingual can have an accent in all of his or her languages. This can happen, for example, when a bilingual has spent her early years going back and forth between two or more linguistic communities (for example, between Germany, Italy, and England). Again, there is nothing wrong with having accents in several languages, although the bilingual may feel that she speaks no language correctly. This is false, of course. Having an accent is not an indication of how well one has mastered a language.

Researchers do not agree on an age limit distinguishing between the likelihood of not having an accent in a second language and having one. Some have proposed that a language can be "accentless" if it is acquired before age six, and that the window (what some call the sensitive period) remains open until age twelve.[1] There are many exceptions, however, including reports of highly motivated people (language teachers, for instance) who have learned a language later but compensated for that disadvantage with intensive contact with native speakers, extended stays in the country in question, the study of phonetics and pronunciation, and so on, and who "pass" as native speakers of the language.[2] Personally, I know individuals who arrived in a new country at age fifteen and even later and yet do not have a foreign accent in that language. And they didn't have to work hard to attain this fluency, they tell me. Despite such accounts, early learning—acquiring a second or third language in early childhood, and using it extensively—is a good guarantee for "accentless" speech. (I put "accentless" in quotes because all speech is accented, by definition, although not in the sense used here.)

Disadvantages and Advantages of Having an Accent

What are the reported disadvantages of having an accent? The one that is mentioned the most is that it makes you stick out from the others when you want the exact opposite, to blend in. Eva Hoffman, author of the much acclaimed *Lost in Translation*, writes about her experience of having an accent during her teenage years:

> Some of my high school peers accuse me of putting it on
> in order to appear more "interesting." In fact, I'd do any-
> thing to get rid of it, and when I'm alone, I practice
> sounds for which my speech organs have no intuitions,
> such as "th" (I do this by putting my tongue between my
> teeth) and "a," which is longer and more open in Polish
> (by shaping my mouth into a sort of arrested grin).[3]

And as an adult, if one's accent is quite strong, and the society is not positively inclined toward the group you belong to, an accent can have a negative effect on the way you are perceived and treated. James Bossard, a sociologist, gives us this example:

> Benjamin . . . has been a traveling salesman. He was
> reared in a Yiddish-speaking home, and he speaks Eng-
> lish today with a remarked Yiddish accent. Benjamin says

81

that this fact handicaps him in selling, particularly in certain areas of the country.[4]

Having an accent may also give the wrong impression—that the speaker does not know the language when he or she does know it, maybe even extremely well. In addition, it may signal that the speaker has not tried hard enough to learn the language, when in fact the accent is the result of neuromuscular factors and not a lack of effort put into language learning. Finally, having an accent does not normally impede communication, but from time to time one can meet a person who has such a strong accent in one of his or her languages that it seems like the person is speaking the other language. Intelligibility suffers, even though the person may be quite fluent in the language. When this happens in a conversation, for example, one can normally find strategies for understanding what is being said. If this is not possible, one may have to shorten the interaction (in as a polite way as possible); fortunately such instances are relatively rare.

An accent can seem odd or startling when a person's name does not match up with his accent. In Switzerland, for example, a person with the very French name Jean-François Guignard may speak French with a German accent. This could simply be because he and his parents (say, a Swiss French father and a Swiss German mother) moved to the German part of Switzerland when he was young and he acquired French rather late in life. People may be taken aback by his accent and wonder why he has it, but it is not that surprising when they know the full story. Another disadvantage to accents that is mentioned by many is that stress and emotion can make an accent reappear or increase in strength. Canadian and French bilingual author Nancy Huston reports that her English accent in

French becomes stronger when she is nervous, when she speaks to strangers, when she has to leave a message on an answering machine, or when she has to speak in public.[5]

Clearly, there are also advantages to having an accent. One is that the accent may be seen positively by a person or a group. Huston writes:

> The minute I detect foreign intonations, my interest and empathy are quickened. Even if I have no direct contact with the person in question . . . my ears prick up when I hear her accent and, studying them unobtrusively, I try to imagine the other, faraway side of her life.[6]

Tony Blair, the former prime minister of the United Kingdom, has a strong English accent in French, but the French love it when he gives speeches in their language, especially as he invariably makes them laugh with his British humor with its irony, innuendo, and deadpan style. Numerous performing artists have played on their accent to appeal to their audience, such as French singer Maurice Chevalier and Italian actor Roberto Benigni when performing in English, and British singers Petula Clark and Jane Birkin when performing in French. I have also known of cases in which an accent was a major factor in a person's falling in love with someone (although not the only factor, one hopes).

Another, slightly less romantic advantage to having an accent is that it clearly marks you as a member of your group. For example, a Swiss person from the French-speaking part of Switzerland speaking German with a French accent is revealing, unconsciously, the group he belongs to. Some people do not want to be seen as belonging to the other language group and purposely use their accent as a signal of their original group membership. Elizabeth

Beaujour, an expert on bilingual writers, writes that the Russian-born French writer Elsa Triolet had a strong Russian accent in French, which embarrassed her. She retained it, however, and Beaujour claims that it was her way of showing that she had not betrayed her linguistic loyalty to Russian, her first language.[7] Finally, having an accent can be self-protective: it prevents members of the group you are interacting with from expecting you to know all the group's cultural and social rules. In short, it allows you to be different.[8]

To summarize, having an accent when you know and use two or more languages is a fact of life; it doesn't make you any less bilingual, and it rarely impedes communication. It is something bilinguals get used to, as do others they interact with.

8

Languages across the Lifespan

In Chapter 2, I stressed how important it is to take into account the language history of bilinguals. To understand an individual bilingual's language knowledge and use, we need to know, for example, which languages, and language skills, were acquired, as well as when and how. Were the languages acquired at the same time—something that is quite rare—or one after the other? We also need to know about the pattern of language fluency and use over the years. Hence, examining how languages wax and wane during a lifetime, which may well include the learning of new languages and the forgetting of older ones, is very much part of understanding the bilingual person.

The Wax and Wane of Languages

To illustrate the language history of bilinguals, I will offer my own case as an example, as it will allow us to see how the waxing and waning of languages is a dynamic process, how language dominance may change over time, and how a bilingual's language history can be quite complex. In Figure 8.1, I present five language use and language fluency grids based on the configuration set up in

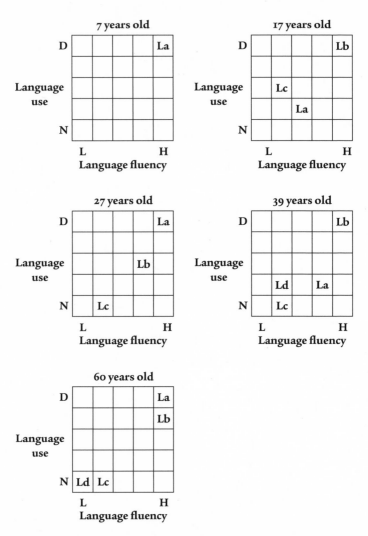

Figure 8.1. The wax and wane of languages in a bilingual. The axis for language use goes from never used (N, bottom) to daily use (D, top), and that for language fluency from low fluency (L, left) to high fluency (H, right). The four languages in question are French (La), English (Lb), Italian (Lc), and American Sign Language (Ld).

Chapter 2. Recall that language use is presented along the vertical axis, on a continuum from never used (N) on the bottom, to daily use (D) on the top, and language fluency is presented along the horizontal axis, from low fluency (L) on the left, to high fluency (H) on the right. Each grid, with the exception of the last one, corresponds to the status of my languages one year before a major language change. The four languages involved are French (La), English (Lb), Italian (Lc), and American Sign Language (Ld).

In the first grid, we see that in my early years (at age seven) I was monolingual in French (La). It is the only language represented on the grid and it is placed in the top right square, which corresponds to daily use and high fluency (for a boy of that age, of course). At eight years of age I was put into an English boarding school in Switzerland, followed by a similar school in England. Hence the appearance of English (Lb) in the second grid, which quickly became my stronger language. I also acquired Italian (Lc) during the months I spent in Italy over the school breaks. So in the second grid (age seventeen), English is the most-used and most-fluent language. I hardly used French at that time and had only medium fluency in it; I used Italian more than French, but my Italian was not quite as fluent.

At age eighteen, a second major linguistic change occurred. I left England and returned to France after an absence of ten years. Overnight, French became my most important language (although it was several years before my fluency improved) and English became the less-used language. So in the third grid (age twenty-seven) French has gone back up to the top right square and English has dropped in fluency and especially in use. As for Italian, it was not being used at all and its fluency was thus also quite low.

Two more linguistic changes took place in my life after that.

When I was twenty-eight my family and I moved to the United States for a one-year stay that was to end up lasting twelve years. The fourth grid (age thirty-nine) shows my language status at the end of that period, just before we returned to Europe. English is back up in the top right position, French has dropped a bit in fluency and even more in use, and Italian remains in the same place. During this period, I also had the privilege of discovering and learning an exceptional language, American Sign Language (Ld), the language used by the Deaf in the United States to communicate among themselves and with signing members of the hearing world. Unfortunately my fluency in ASL was never very high and I didn't use it much (mainly at work), which explains its lower-left position on the grid.

Finally, at age forty, I returned to Europe with my family (to the French-speaking part of Switzerland), and once again my languages reorganized themselves. The final grid, which represents my languages a few years ago (age sixty), is where things stand now, with two highly fluent languages, French and English, the first used slightly more than the second, and two languages, Italian and American Sign Language, that are never used, with Italian slightly more fluent than ASL.

An interested bilingual reader might wish to take a colored pen and fill in the grids in Figure 8.1 for points just before major changes in his or her own language history. One could also examine the fluency and use of each language skill (speaking, listening, reading, writing) at each stage; this would entail filling in four grids per stage.

A few general comments can be made based on my particular language history. (I kept it quite factual for the purpose of illustrating the chapter. Of course, it was also a very human experience with its ups and its downs, especially at age eighteen—but that is another story.) First, as we can see, an individual language history can be quite complex. In my case this was because of repeated immigration. Other bilinguals may have more straightforward histories (for example, those who live on language borders or in multilingual countries), but important life events may nevertheless change the relative importance of their languages—events such as starting school (and learning to read and write in one or several languages), getting a job, settling down with a spouse, or losing a close family member with whom a language was used exclusively.

Second, we see that this is a dynamic process in which new situations, new interlocutors, and new language functions involve new linguistic needs (recall the complementarity principle). New needs will change the bilingual person's language configuration. Typically there are periods of stability, of varying duration, and then periods of language reorganization during which an existing language may be strengthened, another one may lose its importance, yet another may be acquired, and so on. One should be careful not to judge a person's bilingualism during these transition periods, as the skills required by the new environment may not be fully in place. It is also during these periods that bilinguals need to be reassured about what is happening to them. Even if their general level of communication is affected for a while, it will recover as their languages reorganize themselves.

Third, the figure grids show clearly how global dominance in a language can change and how the bilingual's first language is not automatically the stronger language at a particular point in time. In my experience, language dominance changed four times and there were two periods, both about ten years long, when my second language was the dominant language. I have known many bilinguals who have started their lives with one language as the dominant language and then at some point, after a transition, found it replaced by a second language. One should be careful, therefore, not to think that the bilingual's first language, or mother tongue, is the stronger, most fundamental language; it really depends on the individual's language history and, as we have seen, on the complementarity principle. Finally, an examination of bilinguals' language history will help counter another false idea:

Myth: Real bilinguals acquire their two or more languages in childhood.

One can become bilingual in childhood, but also in adolescence and in adulthood. In fact, many people become bilingual as adults, after they immigrate to another region or another country or because they marry someone who speaks another language that becomes the language used in the home. With time, adults can become just as bilingual as those who acquired their languages in their early years, although probably without the native-speaker's accent for some of them.

Language Forgetting

Changes in the life of bilinguals, such as immigration or the loss of a close family member, may be the start of what is sometimes referred to as language loss or language attrition. I will use the better known expression "language forgetting," even though it is not clear whether a language is really forgotten or is simply so deactivated that one can no longer access it correctly. The language researcher Linda Galloway presented a very fine example relating to a heptalingual—someone with seven languages—five of which were in the process of being forgotten at the time of the study. This person first learned Hungarian, followed by Polish at age four when he moved to Poland. He seemed to have "lost" his Hungarian then, until he returned to Hungary at age six. At age ten he moved to Romania, where he learned both Romanian, in school and with friends, and Yiddish, spoken socially. He returned to Hungary at age twelve where, in school, he studied German, English, and Hebrew. He then spent six years in Germany, where he went to college, and German became his dominant language. At age twenty-five he left for the United States, where English became his primary language. His wife is Hungarian but they mainly use English in the home. When Galloway met this person, he was actively using only two languages, English and Hungarian; three were dormant, on the way to being forgotten, German, Hebrew, and Yiddish; and two were all but forgotten, Romanian and Polish.[1]

Language forgetting is a phenomenon that is probably as common as language learning, and yet it has received little attention in the past. This is now changing, thanks to the work of such researchers as Monika Schmid, Barbara Köpke, and Kees de Bot, among others. When the domains of use of a language are considerably reduced, if not simply absent, the process of language forgetting will begin, and it will extend over many years. It can be observed in various ways: in hesitant language production as the bilingual searches for appropriate words or expressions; frequent code-switching, borrowing, and interferences as he or she calls on the dominant language for help; pronunciation (sounds, intonation) that is marked increasingly by the other language or languages; "odd" syntactic structures or expressions that are borrowed from the stronger language, as well as many writing difficulties, particularly in spelling but also at other linguistic levels. Language comprehension is less affected, although the person may not know new words and new colloquialisms in the language that is being forgotten. People who are in this extended process of forgetting a language and are using only one language are "dormant bilinguals." They often avoid using the fading language because they no longer feel sure about their knowledge of it and they do not want to make too many mistakes. If they do have to use it, they may cut short a conversation so as not to have to show openly how far the attrition has progressed. Personally, I try not to use my Italian or my sign language. If I am in situations where there is no other option left, I find myself struggling to express even simple things. I am constantly excusing myself, commenting on how bad my knowledge of a particular language is, falling back whenever I can on my two other languages, or asking others to help me out.

Although people have their lives to live and cannot stop to worry about a language that they are forgetting, in certain contexts, such as with speakers of that language, they become conscious of the "lost" language, and some may feel guilty about it. Hence such remarks as "I really should have kept up my X" or "I wish I could speak X the way I once did." One should keep in mind, though, that language forgetting is simply the flip side of language acquisition (both are governed by the strength of the need for a language) and they are just as interesting linguistically. But the attitudes one has toward them are very different. Whereas language acquisition is seen positively ("Oh, you're learning Spanish, how wonderful!"), language forgetting is not talked about in such terms and those who are losing a language often experience regret if not remorse. These feelings may be even stronger if one's name is linked with the language in question. Hence, an Italian American person with an Italian name may find herself having to explain, and lamenting, the loss of the Italian she no longer ever uses.

Language loss is usually quite a slow process, but bilinguals may sometimes amplify the "damage" observed because the impression it leaves can be so disturbing. In one of her books, author Nancy Huston analyzed the status of her English ten years after moving from Canada to France, where French had become her dominant language. She wrote that she was frightened by the atrophy of her mother tongue. Her vocabulary was much reduced, she observed, and it was only when she read Shakespeare, Joyce, or Djuna Barnes that she rediscovered hundreds of words that were no longer part of her vocabulary. She concluded that, far from having become "perfectly bilingual," she felt doubly "mi-lingue" (semilingual).[2] Of course, even though Huston was going through a dominant French period at that time, she was far from semilingual, even though she felt that this was the case. This is the impression that many have when they see that one of their languages is "withering away." A few years later, Huston started writing novels in English (her first books were in French), and since then she has become one of a few exceptional bilinguals who write prose in both of their languages.

Bilingualism and the Elderly

As the years move on, bilinguals sometimes ask themselves what the status of their language knowledge and use will be in old age, especially in their second language, which may have become their everyday mode of communication. Nancy Huston is married to a Bulgarian-French bilingual, and they use French, his and her second language, as their common language. She evokes this question in a startling but touching way:

> We're sometimes filled with dread at the perspective of a
> quasi-autistic communal old age. At first our acquired

language will desert us bit by bit and our sentences will
be studded with blanks: 'Could you get me the . . . ? You
know, the thing that's hanging from the . . . in the . . . ??!'
. . . Eventually, with French totally erased from our memories, we shall sit in our rocking-chairs from dawn to
dusk, nattering incomprehensibly in our respective
mother tongues.[3]

Robert Schrauf, an expert on aging in bilinguals and biculturals,
reassures all of us who live with two or more languages that the
probability that we will in any way resemble Huston's description is
extremely low. Admittedly, old age has an impact on language perception (poorer speech discrimination, difficulty with more complex or faster speech, poorer storage of the information obtained)
and with language production (word-finding difficulties, especially
proper names), but this is true of both monolinguals and bilinguals. Schrauf states quite clearly that older bilinguals experience
the same kinds of age-related processing deficits as monolinguals,
although he does add that little is known about bilinguals who are
dominant in one language.[4]

Just recently, two studies seem to show that, on the contrary, elderly bilinguals need not worry about being any different from
elderly monolinguals. In the first study, a Canadian specialist in the
cognition of bilinguals, Ellen Bialystok, and her collaborators studied inhibitory control in monolinguals and bilinguals of various
ages, using what is known as the Simon task. The study's older subjects—the ones we are concerned with here—were between the ages
of sixty and eighty. Subjects were asked to look at a computer
screen and to press the response key marked "X" when they saw a red
square and the key marked "O" when they saw a blue square. The

squares appeared either on the left or the right side of the screen. In congruent trials, the red square appeared above the "X" key and the blue square above the "O" key; in the incongruent trials, the red square appeared above the "O" key and the blue square appeared above the "X" key. The authors' findings replicated the well-attested congruency effect: the subjects were faster in responding when the colored square appeared on the same side as its corresponding key (for example, when the red square was on the same side as the "X" key), and slower when the color and the key were not on the same side. This is known as the Simon effect. What is even more interesting, though, is that the bilingual subjects in the older group were faster than a matched monolingual group, on both the congruent and the incongruent trials.[5] In a control study, the authors ruled out the possibility that the speed difference was due to baseline differences between the groups.

The authors' explanation for the elderly bilinguals' advantage was that the need to manage two active language systems, and to manipulate attention to one or the other, or both, during language use, is carried out by the same general executive (cognitive) functions that are responsible for managing attention to any set of systems or stimuli. In other words, a lifetime of activities such as language choice, which forces bilinguals to activate one language and deactivate (maybe even inhibit) the other, at least in the monolingual mode, has given them an attentional advantage in the kinds of tasks in which you have to pay attention to one cue (the color of the square) and not another (where it is located). Bilinguals seem to have a head start, and this can be observed in bilingual children too (which we will address in Part 2).

The second study, also conducted by Ellen Bialystok and her collaborators, has received much attention in the popular press, as it shows that being bilingual may well delay the development of dementia in old age. Dementia is a general term applied to cognitive disorders that have an impact on memory, language, motor and spatial skills, problem solving, and attention. Alzheimer's disease is the most common cause of dementia; others include brain injury, brain tumors, and so on. The authors examined 184 patients diagnosed with dementia, 51 percent of whom were bilingual. The latter were fluent in English (the language of the monolinguals) as well as another language (in all, they represented twenty-five different languages). The bilingual subjects had spent the majority of their lives, at least from early adulthood, regularly using both languages. When the authors compared the age of onset of the symptoms of dementia in the two groups, they found that the bilinguals had a mean age of onset 4.1 years *later* than the monolinguals (at 75.5 years versus 71.4 years). The authors argue, once again, that the attentional control that bilinguals use to govern their languages—choosing one or the other or both, keeping one suppressed while activating the other (at least when communicating in the monolingual mode)—is akin to other complex mental activities that appear to protect against dementia. They conclude tentatively (the findings are still recent) that while bilingualism does not appear to affect the accumulation of pathological factors associated with dementia, it enables the brain to better tolerate the accumulated pathologies.[6]

Growing old as a bilingual does not seem to be very different from growing old as a monolingual, with its advantages and disadvantages; it may just be, though, that bilinguals have a few additional cognitive benefits in their favor.

9

Attitudes and Feelings about Bilingualism

Almost everyone has something to say about bilingualism. Here are extracts from the testimonies of three bilinguals:

> Dutch-English bilingual: "You are able to communicate with people in different countries."

> American Sign Language–English bilingual: "Bilingualism gives you a double perspective on the world."

> German-French-English trilingual: "There is the advantage of being able to read a greater variety of books, of traveling, and of conversing with people directly."[1]

We will start with a closer examination of the perceptions of bilinguals themselves (positive and negative) and then move on to how monolinguals see bilingualism.

How Bilinguals View the Advantages of Bilingualism

One major point that comes up often is the ability bilinguals have to communicate with different people of different cultures and in different countries.[2] It is certainly true that being bilingual allows you to interact with many different people, especially if the languages you use are major world languages. It is also the case that if one does not master a language sufficiently well, or at all, communication can be very difficult. When the Italian soccer coach Fabio Capello was appointed to be England's national coach, many in the media asked how he would be able to communicate with his players as his English was limited. He was reported to have said things like, "At this moment, my English is not so well" and "I am very proud and hon-or-ried."[3] He stated that he would study English intensively, but members of the press were dubious. (I am happy to report that a few months later he had made good progress.) On a more serious note, there is the story of Mario Capecchi, a Nobel Prize winner for medicine, who at age seventy was reunited with his half-sister, Marlene Bonelli, age sixty-nine, whom he had not seen since World War II, some sixty years earlier. He had been separated from his mother and sister during the war and had had to fend for himself in very difficult circumstances while his mother was interned in the Dachau concentration camp. His mother and he were finally reunited in 1946 and they moved to the United States, but without his half-sister, who was at this point in Austria. Capecchi and his sister only saw each other again in 2008, under very moving circumstances. The problem was, they had no common language— his sister did not speak English and he didn't speak German, his sister's main language.

Linked to the ability to communicate with more people is the fact that bilingualism allows one to read more books (if one is literate in several languages, of course) and, for some bilinguals, it allows for greater clarity in speaking and a richer vocabulary. Another linguistic advantage is that knowing several languages seems to help you learn other languages. Many bilinguals have reported on this and the claim makes sense. First there is the fact that new languages may be related to the ones already known and this will facilitate learning (knowing French will help you learn Spanish, knowing Dutch will facilitate the learning of German), and there is also the fact that the human mind structures languages—their phonology, morphology, syntax, and so on—in such a way that links are created between them. These links, in turn, can be a real help in the acquisition and use of a new language.

Bilingualism also seems to encourage divergent thinking. It has often been reported that bilingual children are able to distance themselves from the form of a word rather early on and can appreciate that something may be named in many different ways and serve different purposes. Besides the cognitive advantages for older bilinguals, mentioned in the previous chapter, bilingualism has cognitive benefits for adults across the board. In one study, researcher Anatoliy Kharkhurin asked bilinguals and monolinguals to undertake various tasks, such as imagining difficult situations and identifying the troubles they might encounter, or drawing pictures with incomplete figures or with triangles. From these he obtained various measures of fluency, originality, elaboration, and flexibility. He concluded that bilinguals were superior in divergent thinking tasks that require the ability to simultaneously activate and process multiple unrelated concepts from distant categories. The bilingual subjects were superior to monolinguals in three of the measures, fluency, elaboration, and flexibility; the one area in which they behaved identically to monolinguals was originality, that is, the ability to produce uncommon ideas or ideas that are totally new or unique.[4]

The social and cultural dimension of bilingualism is often mentioned as a real advantage for those who know and use more than one language in everyday life. Bilingualism is reported to foster open-mindedness, offer different perspectives on life, and reduce cultural ignorance. A more instrumental advantage is also mentioned: bilingualism may lead to more job opportunities and greater social mobility, and may also be a real advantage in one's current occupation. I have known people who were offered a particular job, or new responsibilities, precisely because they knew one or two additional languages. In a large European Union survey conducted in twenty-nine countries in 2006, the job factor was mentioned many times in respondents' answers to the question, "What would be your main reasons for learning a new language?" A third of the respondents answered, "To use at work (including traveling abroad on business)" and a fourth indicated, "To be able to work in another country" and "To get a better job in your own country."[5]

Other advantages put forward for being bilingual are that it allows one to help others, it creates a bond with other bilinguals, and it sometimes allows one to understand what others may not. The final report on the European Union survey summarizes many of the advantages given above:

> The benefits of knowing foreign languages are unquestionable. Language is the path to understanding other ways of living which in turn opens up the space for intercultural tolerance. Furthermore, language skills facilitate working, studying and traveling . . . and allow intercultural communication.[6]

I was touched when I received this testimony from a German-French-English trilingual who, in a few lines, said it all so well:

> Being a trilingual has helped me in various ways. I have
> achieved greater stature in my work environment; I have
> developed my lingual capacities; I have become more
> open-minded toward minorities and more aware of their
> linguistic problems; I have enjoyed various forms of liter-
> ature and felt a certain amount of pride in being able to
> read in three different languages . . . Life never becomes
> boring, because there is more than just one language
> available. Being trilingual has been a guide to under-
> standing and helping others.

All the advantages cited above are important for daily life, and quality of life, and show clearly why it is crucial to encourage and foster bilingualism. But they can never compare with such exceptional moments as when lives were spared precisely because of bilingualism. Here are two examples. A Bengali-Urdu-English trilingual once told me that when Bangladesh had its war of independence in 1971 against Pakistan, he was arrested by a Pakistani Punjabi/Urdu platoon one day and was on the verge of being shot. Although Bengali himself, he managed to be released because he showed his captors that he could speak Urdu and that he could recite a few verses of the Koran in Arabic. The second example concerns August Bohny, a Swiss citizen who was recognized as Righteous among the Nations by the State of Israel for having risked his life to save Jews during the Holocaust. Bohny was a primary-school teacher who worked for the Red Cross in World War II. He went to France to set up homes for parentless children, many of them Jewish, who had been taken out of internment camps. One morning, the pro-German Vichy police came to his house and asked him to give up the Jewish children he was hosting (twelve of them were sleeping right there in the dining room). Bohny spoke good French (he was Swiss German) and managed to delay things by convincing the officers to go back to the village to phone their headquarters. While they were away, he roused the children and quickly sent them out to the farms that surrounded the village. When the police came back, Bohny told them that the children were gone. His own suitcase was ready, as he thought he would be taken to prison, but nothing came of it and he managed to continue his exemplary work until the end of the war.

How Bilinguals View the Inconveniences of Bilingualism

According to the bilingual individuals I surveyed, the inconveniences of bilingualism are less numerous than the advantages. In fact, when I asked a group of bilinguals and trilinguals what the disadvantages were, 52 percent of the bilinguals and 67 percent of the trilinguals replied that there weren't any.[7] That said, there are some negative aspects that I will mention.

First, bilinguals who do not know one of their languages well sometimes report that they get tired and frustrated having to use it (speaking or writing) and that they invariably make mistakes when doing so. The author Richard Rodriguez mentions this aspect in his book *Hunger of Memory,* when recounting how his Spanish-speaking father dealt with English in his family:

> Though his English improved somewhat, he retired into
> silence. At dinner he spoke very little. One night his chil-
> dren and even his wife helplessly giggled at his garbled
> English pronunciation of the Catholic Grace before
> Meals. Thereafter, he made his wife recite the prayer at

> the start of each meal, even on formal occasions when
> there were guests in the house. Hers became the public
> voice of the family.[8]

Rodriguez tells us that his father was not shy but that he simply didn't master English as well as Spanish; when speaking the latter, he would convey a confidence and authority not expressed in English.

Another disadvantage bilinguals mention concerns the influence of their stronger language on a weaker one. Some bilinguals report that, when speaking monolingually, they often have to struggle to keep code-switches and borrowings out and they have to put up with interferences that increase in number as they get tired, nervous, angry, or worried. In fact, the fear of having languages "contaminate" one another has pushed a few people not to learn or use another language at all, even when their environment encourages them to do so. A good example is that of the French writer, poet, and surrealist André Breton, who spent time in the United States during World War II (he worked for the U.S. Office of War Information). He is reported to have refused to speak and write in English, although his passive knowledge of the language was good. The reason he gave was that he didn't want his French to be affected by English. Bilinguals are rarely as puristic as Breton, but it is true that some are particularly careful not to let interferences seep through; this leads to careful, sometimes hesitant speech that sounds almost abnormal in its correctness.

Some bilinguals report difficulties adapting to new situations and new environments that require more of one language and less of the other (see the complementarity principle). They feel they don't have time to adjust, and they struggle with the language that is suddenly thrust to the forefront. Any bilingual who, after even a short journey, has suddenly had to adjust to a new language environment will sympathize with this. Similarly, having to speak in public can be very trying if it has to be done in the "wrong" language—either the weaker language or the language not normally used in formal situations.

Another inconvenience mentioned by bilinguals is that they are often asked to act as interpreters or translators, and many find this both difficult and tiring (as I discussed earlier). Since they may not want to refuse a favor asked of them, they often struggle through the job but then report how stressful it was. The situation can be even more difficult if a bilingual has to serve as intermediary between two cultures when he or she is personally involved. Paul Preston, who interviewed a number of English-ASL bilinguals, sons and daughters of Deaf parents, gives us the vivid testimony of a person who had to interpret at her father's funeral because there was nobody else who could do it:

> I didn't want to do it . . . but I had to. For Mamma. There
> wasn't anybody else. I just kept sobbing and signing, all
> mixed up, all at the same time. [signs, "*Never again.*"] I
> never want to do anything like that again."[9]

One disadvantage that we will return to in the next chapter is that some bilinguals who are also bicultural do not feel they belong to any cultural group. They feel estranged from their cultures, particularly at turning points in their lives (for example, when they return "home," which is no longer home).

Despite these pluses and minuses, I asked bilinguals if they felt they were any different from monolinguals. In general, they answered that they did not, except for the fact that they have more languages and hence can communicate with more people.

Bilingualism as Seen by Monolinguals

The attitudes and feelings that monolinguals have toward bilinguals, and bilingualism, are extremely varied. They range from the very positive to the very negative. The world expert on bilingualism, Einar Haugen, stated this in the following way back in 1972, and what he said is still relevant today in many places:

> Bilingualism is a term that evokes mixed reactions nearly
> everywhere. On the one hand, some people . . . will say,
> "How wonderful to be bilingual!" On the other, they
> warn parents, "Don't make your child bilingual."[10]

Not only is there a difference of opinion regarding adult bilinguals as opposed to child bilinguals, but there is especially a difference regarding bilinguals of a higher socioeconomic status as opposed to bilinguals of a lower status, primarily those who are immigrants or members of a minority language group. Whereas the former impress monolinguals with their ability to master languages and to move freely from one language to another, the latter are seen more negatively, particularly if they speak the dominant language with an accent and have children who are having difficulties adapting in their monolingual school. Many of the myths that are discussed in this book emanate from this latter monolingual view of the bilingual person.

Unlike smaller European countries and countries in Africa and Asia where multilingualism is the norm, the United States and other large nations such as England and France have not been very supportive of their inhabitants who live their lives with two or more languages. Here is what linguist Barry McLaughlin said about this some while back, in 1978:

> In the United States, monolingualism traditionally has been the norm. Bilingualism was regarded as a social stigma and a liability . . . This hostility toward bilingualism has nothing to do with language as such. The hostility is directed not at language but at culture. The bilingual represents an alien way of thinking and alien values.[11]

Have things changed since then? In fact attitudes and feelings simply do not change that fast, as Aneta Pavlenko, a contemporary researcher in bilingualism and herself an immigrant to the United States, attests. She writes that bilinguals are often viewed with suspicion either as linguistic and cultural hybrids who may be in conflict with themselves, or as individuals whose shifting linguistic allegiances imply shifting political allegiances and moral commitments.[12]

The immigrant literature is unfortunately rife with examples of discrimination against immigrants who are also bilingual. I have always personally regretted that large, rather monolingual countries have not fostered the bilingualism of their minorities, immigrant or not. Government-sponsored reports come out every so often lamenting a country's incompetence in second and foreign languages, which, in this age of worldwide contact, has become a serious liability. The paradox, of course, is that there *are* many speakers of second languages in these large countries, but they are not the ones in positions of power where the languages are needed. Millions of dollars are injected into the teaching of second languages to monolinguals when second-language skills already exist within many minority groups. Were we to support and cultivate this important national resource, as well as encourage the learning of second languages, we would be on the way to solving the foreign-languages problem that many decry.

In the end, the more monolingual a group or country is, the more difficult it is for the society to understand that bilinguals are a real asset to a nation in terms of what they can bring to cross-cultural communication and understanding.

10

Bilinguals Who Are Also Bicultural

Since language is a part of culture and learning a new language may sometimes mean acquiring a new culture, many people share the following false impression of bilinguals:

Myth: Bilinguals are also bicultural.

In fact bilingualism is not coextensive with biculturalism. Many people use two or more languages in everyday life while belonging to just one main culture. For example, a Dutch person may use Dutch, English, and German in everyday life but really only live within the Dutch culture. Hence being bilingual does not automatically mean that one is also bicultural. That said, many bilinguals *are* also bicultural—and these bicultural bilinguals are the subject of this chapter.

Describing Bicultural People

Culture reflects all the facets of life of a group of people: their social rules, their behaviors, their beliefs, their values, their customs and traditions. As individuals, we belong to a number of cultures (often called cultural networks) made up of minor and major cultures. Minor cultures include the ones related to specific areas of life, such as one's job, habitat, sports, hobbies, whereas major cultures encompass the national culture of the country we live in, the social and religious groups we belong to, and so on. In a way, we are all "multicultural," and our cultural networks are usually complementary in the sense that we can belong to several at a time. In what follows, we will look at biculturalism as it pertains to major cultures, most notably national or ethnic groups that, in our case, also have different languages. I am interested in the fact that some people are both French and Italian, German and American, Kurdish and Turkish, Russian and Estonian, even though some of these pairings are frowned upon or even rejected by the individual groups in question.

How can one describe people who are bicultural? They have the following characteristics: first, they take part, to varying degrees, in the life of two or more cultures. For instance, Koreans in the United States take part in the life of their Korean community in America as well as that of the larger American society. Second, they adapt, at least in part, their attitudes, behavior, values, and languages to their cultures. Hence, Koreans in the United States adapt their language and their behavior depending on whether they are with other Koreans or with members of the larger American society. And third, they combine and blend aspects of the cultures involved. Certain aspects (beliefs, values, attitudes, behaviors, and so on) come from one or the other culture—hence statements like, "That's my Korean side" or "That's my American side"—whereas other aspects are blends of the two cultures. An example here would be facial expressions and body language, which are often the product of both cultures blended into one unique configuration.[1]

Thus biculturals will adapt to certain situations or contexts (this is a dynamic, adaptable component of their biculturalism) while also blending some features of their two cultures (this part is not as readily adaptable). Here is how a Franco-American describes his own biculturalism, most notably the blending aspect:

> To me, being bilingual in the U.S. and, more specifically, being Franco-American in our pluralistic society, means that I have two languages, two heritages, two ways of thinking and viewing the world. At times these two elements may be separate and distinct within me, whereas at other times they are fused together.[2]

Figure 10.1 depicts an example of one person's biculturalism. We see the two cultures, represented by squares (here culture A is dominant) and the component that blends certain aspects of the two cultures, represented by the oval. Cultures rarely have exactly the same importance for the bicultural person; one culture often plays a larger role, and so we can speak of cultural dominance in the same way that we speak of language dominance in bilinguals (but

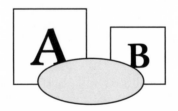

Figure 10.1. A bicultural person's combination of two cultures (culture A, the dominant culture, and culture B), along with the blending component (shaded oval).

this dominance does not make a person any less bicultural). In the illustration, we see by the relative size of the squares that culture A is more important than culture B. In a bicultural's lifetime, cultures can wax and wane, become dominant for a while before taking a secondary role. In my own case, I feel that I have changed my dominant culture four times since becoming bicultural: it was English in my teenage years, French until age twenty-eight, American until I was forty, and it has been Swiss since then.

People can become bicultural at any time during their life: in childhood, when a child is born into a bicultural family; when a child starts going to school; in adolescence, if the young person moves from one culture to another; and, of course, in adulthood, as with immigrants who settle down in a new country and, over the years, become bicultural. Concerning the latter, the stages that take place in migration are now well studied—arrival, isolation, culture shock, and more or less rapid acculturation. This last stage is affected by the size and concentration of the migrant group, the number of children in the family, the host country's attitude toward the group in question, and so on. The literature also mentions the migrants' idealization of their home country, the return shock they experience when they see that "back home" no longer matches their dreams and memories, and the more or less permanent acceptance of a migratory status. Nancy Huston writes:

> As time goes by, your communications with "back home"
> become fewer and farther between . . . Your parents age,
> your siblings change jobs and/or spouses, have children,
> remarry, redivorce, you can't keep up with it all . . . The
> foreigners who surrounded you when you first arrived . . .

have become your compatriots. Now it is *their* destiny
that means the most to you, because it has become *your*
destiny.[3]

Biculturals can be involved in more than two major cultures, depending on their life's itinerary. Figure 10.2 depicts a tricultural
who is currently dominant in culture B; her next most important
culture is C, and then culture A.

Acting Biculturally

Bilinguals who are also bicultural may find themselves at various
points along a situational continuum that requires different types
of behavior depending on their situation. At one end they are in a
monocultural mode, since they are with monoculturals or with
biculturals with whom they share only one culture. In this situation they must deactivate as best they can their other cultures. At
the other end of the continuum they are with other biculturals
who share their cultures. With them, they will use a base culture to
interact in (the behaviors, attitudes, beliefs of one culture) and

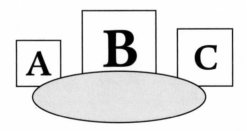

Figure 10.2. The relative importance of the three cultures of a tricultural
person (culture B is dominant, followed by C, then A).

bring in the other culture, in the form of cultural switches and borrowings, when they choose to.

Let us look at the two endpoints a bit more closely. Concerning the monocultural mode, bicultural people in this mode attempt to apply the motto, "When in Rome, do as the Romans do." If their knowledge of the culture in question is sufficient (a bit like having sufficient knowledge of a language that has to be used), and they manage to deactivate, at least to a large degree, their other cultures, then they can behave appropriately. Thus, many biculturals will know how to adapt to such situations as welcoming acquaintances at home, holding a meeting at work, dealing with relatives who are monocultural, doing business with the local administration, dressing according to the context, and so on.

However, because of the blending component in biculturalism, certain behaviors, attitudes, and feelings may not be totally adapted to a situation and may instead be a mixture of the person's two (or more) cultures. This form of static cultural interference is a differentiating factor between bilingualism and biculturalism: bilinguals can usually deactivate one language and use only the other in particular situations, whereas biculturals cannot always deactivate certain traits of their other culture when in a monocultural environment. Let me give a few examples. My greeting behavior is not totally monocultural when it should be, despite my efforts to behave in the right way in each of the four cultures I interact with. When in England, I have a tendency to shake hands at the end of a visit when a small wave would be sufficient (shaking hands takes place at the beginning of an encounter, usually, and is not repeated at the end). Kissing when greeting women friends is also problematic: whom to kiss, and how many times? Just think about it: in England and the United States, if kissing is appropriate at all, it consists of one brief air kiss; in France, you kiss someone on both cheeks; and in Switzerland, you kiss them three times. Things get even more complex when you meet a Swiss friend in France. (Should it be two kisses, the French way, or three, the Swiss way?) Finally, when trying to attract a waiter's attention in a French café, I just can't bring myself to be quite as conspicuous as the normal French customer. Instead of saying, "Garçon!" with a loudish voice, I try to attract the waiter's attention through eye contact and by raising my hand meekly (which invariably leads to failure, at least for the first few tries).

All biculturals who are reading this can add their favorite examples of cultural blends in domains such as the hand gestures to use with someone, the amount of space to leave between yourself and the other, what to talk about (in some cultures, for example, you don't talk about salaries with people you don't know), how much to tip, and so on. Paul Preston, who has interviewed a number of bilingual-bicultural people who have Deaf parents, mentions that prolonged eye contact, something crucial in Deaf culture, makes hearing people feel uncomfortable and hence they try not to use it that much with them.[4] Another example concerns the complicated *tu* versus *vous* form of address in French. An English-French bicultural friend related something that happened to her as she was adapting to the French way of life:

> I once shocked my friends at a small dinner party by using the familiar "tu" form of address to one of the guests, a girl roughly my own age. She was introduced to me as a friend by my host, who was a good friend of mine, and so I thought I should treat her as a potential friend. I was quite unaware of the embarrassment my behavior was

causing the other guests; it was only when she left that the others asked me why I had been so insulting to her. Hadn't I noticed that everyone else said "vous" to her? I realized that the relationships covered by their term "amie" and my unconscious translation "friend" were not equivalent. For me a friend is someone to be friendly with, whereas one may not necessarily be "amical" with an "amie."[5]

Biculturals will invariably say that life is easier when they are in a bicultural mode—that is, with other biculturals like themselves. Bilingualism expert Aneta Pavlenko, herself a Russian-English bilingual-bicultural person, sent me the following example:

Russian-American teenagers in Philadelphia may spend Friday evening with their families laughing over an ever popular Soviet-era comedy and then go out Sunday night to see a new Hollywood blockbuster. Chatting about the movie in English, they may slip in a few Russian adjectives or a reference to a popular character from a Russian movie.[6]

The bicultural teenagers know that the others are intimate with both of their languages and cultures and that they will understand when they intermix the cultures in their behavior or in what they say. These are precious moments, when the bicultural person can relax and not have to worry about getting things right each time. Bicultural bilinguals often state that their good friends (or their "dream" partners) are people like them, with whom they can be totally relaxed about going back and forth between their languages and cultures.

The Bicultural's Identity

One important aspect of biculturalism relates to the identity bicultural people decide to take on. Their dilemma is that monocultural members of their different cultures want to know if they are members of culture A or culture B, or of a new culture, when biculturals just want to be accepted—consciously or unconsciously—for who they are: members of two or more cultures. But reaching a point where one can say, "I am bicultural, a member of culture A *and* of culture B" takes a long time and sometimes never happens.[7] Why is that? The process is dual: there is the way members of the cultures you belong to categorize you, and there is the way you categorize yourself. Others will take into account your kinship, the languages you speak and how well you do so, your physical appearance, your nationality, your education, your attitudes, and so on. The outcome, in each culture you belong to, will often be categorical: you are judged by friends, acquaintances, and others to belong to culture A or to culture B, but rarely to both cultures. An additional problem can be that culture A may categorize you as a member of culture B and vice versa, a form of double, contradictory categorization. Examples of this can be found among young second-generation immigrants in Europe today. Those who stayed behind in the home country categorize those who emigrated as Westerners or Europeans, whereas many citizens of the "host nations" see them as members of their parents' original culture. Young North Africans in France, for example, often feel that they are rejected by both the country of their parents and the country where they were born (France). When they return to Algeria or Tunisia or Morocco, they are treated like foreigners with radical ideas and Western morals, and yet in France they are considered as Arab foreigners and are often discriminated against: their identification papers are checked frequently, they are often mistreated by the police, and they are sometimes threatened with deportation.

Faced with such sometimes contradictory perceptions, biculturals have to reach a decision regarding their own cultural identity. They take into account how they are seen by the cultures they belong to, as well as such other factors as their personal history, their identity needs, their knowledge of the languages and cultures involved, the country they live in, the groups they belong to. The outcome, after a long and sometimes trying process, is to identify solely with culture A, solely with culture B, with neither culture A nor culture B, or with both culture A and culture B.[8] The first three solutions—that is, only A, only B, neither A nor B—are often unsatisfactory in the long run, even if they might be temporary answers. They do not truly reflect the bicultural person who has roots in two cultures, and they may have negative consequences later on. Those who choose to identify with just one culture (whether freely or when pushed to do so) are basically turning away from one of their two cultures, and they may later become dissatisfied with their decision. As for those who reject both cultures, they often feel marginalized or ambivalent about their life. Hence the terms and expressions that abound concerning immigrants and other biculturals, such as "uprooted," "rootless," "hybrid," "neither here nor there," "threshold people." When Paul Preston interviewed bilingual and bicultural hearing children of Deaf parents, he found several who couldn't (or didn't dare) call themselves bicultural, even though their experience was the epitome of biculturalism. One person said:

> I always felt like I didn't belong either place. I didn't be-
> long with the Deaf 100 per cent and I didn't belong with
> the Hearing. I didn't feel comfortable with Hearing. I felt
> more comfortable with Deaf but I knew I wasn't deaf. I
> feel like I'm somewhere in-between.[9]

The fourth route, where one identifies with both cultures, A and B, is the optimal solution since biculturals live their lives within two cultures, combining and blending aspects of each one, even when one culture is dominant. Some biculturals are helped by the existence of new cultural groups, such as the immigrant groups in North America. Identifying with Cuban Americans, or Haitian Americans, for example, and being able to use those labels, is a fine way of telling others that you are of dual heritage, Cuban *and* American or Haitian *and* American, and that you wish to be recognized as a bicultural individual.

For isolated biculturals, finally identifying with both cultures and admitting openly to being bicultural (and not simply neither A nor B, as many biculturals say) may take time or may actually never be possible. In his autobiography, Olivier Todd, the Franco-British journalist and writer, clearly shows throughout his book *Carte d'identités* that he has been in search of his dual and combined identity, despite the fact that when he was a young man French philosopher and writer Jean-Paul Sartre once told him that his problem was that he was divided between England and France. Todd applauds projects between the two countries, such as the Channel Tunnel, and he feels most comfortable with people who have his dual heritage—his mother, his first wife, Anne-Marie, and many bicultural friends. Even though he never actually uses the term "bicultural" (but then, how many biculturals do?), one clearly feels that this is what he aspires to be openly, even though he states that he is slightly more French than English. (Dominance of one culture should in no way be a barrier to accepting one's own biculturalism, although it is for some.) In a very touching part of his book, Todd speaks to Aurélia, his newly adopted little girl of Indian origin:

> "I hope to come back [to India] with you, Aurélia, when
> you'll be . . . twenty or twenty-five years old . . . I'd like
> you to be proud to be French *and* Indian."[10]

I had the privilege of meeting Olivier Todd just before I wrote this book, and I asked him about his biculturalism. I stressed the fact that one could be both A and B even if one culture is dominant. He very kindly responded that I was right and that he was, indeed, bicultural.

The writer Veronica Chambers relates how she progressively discovered her dual identity and how a trip to Panama allowed her to go "from being a lone Black girl with a curious Latin heritage to being part of the Latinegro tribe or the Afro-Antillianos." She continues:

> I was thrilled to learn there was actually a society for peo-
> ple like me. Everyone was Black, everyone spoke Spanish
> and everyone danced the way they danced at fiesta time
> back in Brooklyn.[11]

A counseling psychologist, Teresa LaFromboise, and her colleagues propose that there are six factors that help biculturals accept and live fully in their biculturalism: having a good understanding of the two cultures involved, having a positive attitude toward both, feeling confident that one can live effectively in the two, being able to communicate verbally and nonverbally in the two cultures, knowing what culturally appropriate behavior to use in each, and having a well-developed social network in the two cultures.[12]

I end this chapter on a personal note. When I talk or write about biculturalism, some tell me that I am being too optimistic and that "things are not that easy." Having gone through the struggle of becoming bicultural, I agree with the latter point and do not pretend that the road is without obstacles. I also reply, though, that many biculturals do not receive sufficient help to attain—and accept—their dual identity. Despite this, some come to an acceptance of their biculturalism, even though the two cultures they belong to may not accept them as such. Bicultural people are invaluable in today's world—they are bridges between the cultures they belong to, useful go-betweens who can explain one culture to members of the other and act as intermediaries between the two. As one of Paul Preston's interviewees said, "We can see both sides because we're on both sides."[13]

II

Personality, Thinking and Dreaming, and Emotions in Bilinguals

In Chapter 3, I mentioned how bilinguals deal with well-learned mental processes such as counting, praying, remembering phone numbers, and so on. In this chapter, we will examine some other topics that often come up regarding bilinguals. Do they change personality when they change language? What language do they think in or dream in? And how do they express their emotions? Such questions are fascinating, as are the answers.

The Personality of Bilinguals

In a news item on 24 June 2008 entitled "Switching Languages Can Also Switch Personality: Study," Reuters reported on research that supposedly showed that "people who are bicultural and speak two languages may unconsciously change their personality when they switch languages."[1] With this wire, the international press agency was simply perpetuating a long-standing misapprehension:

> *Myth: Bilinguals have double or split personalities.*

What evidence is there for this position? Before describing the study mentioned by Reuters, let's look at what some individual bilinguals have said about this.[2] A French-English bilingual once wrote to me:

> I know that I am more aggressive, more caustic, when I speak French. I am also more rigid and more narrow-minded in defending my assertions.

A Greek-English bilingual noted:

> In English my speech is very polite, with a relaxed tone, always saying "please" and "excuse me." When I speak Greek, I start talking more rapidly, with a tone of anxiety and in a kind of rude way, without using any English speech characteristics.

Finally, a Russian-English bilingual wrote:

> I find when I'm speaking Russian I feel like a much more gentle, "softer" person. In English, I feel more "harsh," "businesslike."

Thus, both the French-English and the Greek-English bilinguals feel they are more aggressive and more tense in French or Greek, respectively, than they are in English, and the Russian-English bilingual is more gentle in Russian.

The impressions shared by these bilinguals and others have been alluded to in the literature. Robert Di Pietro, a linguist who was himself an English-Italian bilingual, once observed that in an Italian American–owned store in Washington, D.C., the butcher's style was different when he changed languages. In English, he was rather formal, whereas in Italian he would joke and sometimes even engage in mild flirtations with young women.[3] And Charles Gallagher, an expert on North Africa, reported that when Arab French bilinguals enjoyed themselves with French friends, their whole character was quite distinct from that expressed in Arabic.[4]

Psychologist Susan Ervin did some very interesting work at the beginning of her career on this precise question. In one study, she showed Thematic Apperception Test (TAT) cards—cards showing pictures that have ambiguous content—to French-English bilinguals who had lived in the United States for an average of twelve years. She tested them in two sessions, one for each language, that were conducted six weeks apart, and she found significant effects of language on three variables: verbal aggression toward peers, withdrawal-autonomy, and achievement. For example, for the same card one bilingual said in the French-language session,

> I think he [the husband] wants to leave her because he's
> found another woman he loves more . . . I don't know
> whose fault it is but they certainly seem angry.

And in the English-language session she said,

> He's decided to get a good education . . . he keeps on
> working and going to college at night some of the time
> . . . He'll . . . get a better job and they will be much happier . . . his wife will have helped him along.

Ervin observed that in French, the picture elicited themes such as aggression and striving for autonomy, whereas in English the wife is seen as supporting her husband.[5] In another study, Ervin asked Japanese-American women to complete the sentences she gave them in both Japanese and in English. She found that they proposed very different endings, depending on the language used.

For example, for the sentence beginning, "When my wishes conflict with my family . . ." one participant's Japanese ending was, ". . . it is a time of great unhappiness," whereas the English ending was, ". . . I do what I want." For the sentence beginning, "Real friends should . . . " the Japanese ending was, ". . . help each other" and the English ending was, ". . . be very frank."[6]

Some forty years later, David Luna and his colleagues conducted the study that was described by the Reuters newswire. Although very similar to the Ervin studies, the earlier work was not mentioned—which is unfortunate, as Ervin had given a reasonable explanation for the results she had obtained. In Luna's research, Hispanic American bilingual women students were asked to perform several tasks. In one study, they had to interpret target advertisements, first in one language and then, six months later, in another. The ads contained pictures of women, and they were asked questions like, "What is the woman in the ad doing?" "How does she feel?" and so on. Luna and his colleagues found that in the Spanish sessions, informants perceived women in the ads as more self-sufficient (strong, intelligent, industrious, ambitious) as well as extroverted. In the English sessions, however, they voiced a more traditional, other-dependent and family-oriented view of the women. In a second study, the subjects were given a timed categorization task that showed that the associations between the category "masculine" and the category "other-dependent," on the one hand, and the category "feminine" and the category "self-sufficient," on the other, were stronger in Spanish than in English, thereby giving converging evidence for the results of the first study.[7]

Does this mean, then, that bilinguals have two identities, as the title of the Luna paper, "One Individual, Two Identities," seems to indicate? Or that the Reuters statement in its wire based on this re-

search is correct: biculturals who speak two languages may unconsciously change their personality when they switch languages?
Could it be that there is some truth to the Czech proverb, "Learn a
new language and get a new soul"? One should note first that
monocultural bilinguals are not concerned by any of this, even
though they probably make up the vast majority of bilinguals in
the world. Indeed, in many African, European, and Asian nations,
people are bi- or multilingual while being members of just one major culture. But what about bicultural bilinguals? I proposed more
than twenty-five years ago, in my first book on bilingualism, that
what is seen as a change in personality is simply a shift in attitudes
and behaviors corresponding to a shift in situation or context, independent of language.[8] In essence, the bicultural bilingual subjects in these various studies were behaving biculturally—that is,
adapting to the context they were in (see the previous chapter). In
fact Susan Ervin, in her very first study (1964), stated something
similar:

> It is possible that a shift in language is associated with a
> shift in social roles and emotional attitudes. Since each
> language is learned and usually employed with different
> persons and in a different context, the use of each lan-
> guage may come to be associated with a shift in a large
> array of behavior.[9]

As we saw in the earlier discussion of the functions of languages,
bilinguals use their languages for different purposes, in different
domains of life, with different people. Different aspects of life often
require different languages. Contexts and domains trigger different
attitudes, impressions, and behaviors, and what is seen as a personality change due to language shift may have nothing to do with the

language itself. In fact, when I questioned some other bilinguals, they put their finger right on the explanation. A French-Flemish-English trilingual stated:

> I don't really know if my personality changes when I change language. The main reason for this uncertainty is that I use the two languages in different situations and therefore I would act differently even if it was in the same language.

As this trilingual person clearly indicates, different situations make one behave differently, whether one is using one language or several languages. Just think of the way you speak with your best friend, and the behavior and personality you adopt with him or her, and think of how this changes in the most formal interactions you have, such as with a school head, religious authority, or employer. Another way of examining this is to observe biculturals who are monolingual. Although they have just one language, they probably behave exactly like biculturals who are bilingual, thereby demonstrating that it is not a switch in language that triggers behavioral and attitudinal changes.

A final testimony comes from a Swiss German–French–English trilingual:

> When talking English, French, or German to my sister, my personality does not change. However, depending on where we are, both our behaviors may adapt to certain situations we find ourselves in.

In other words, it is the environment and the interlocutors together that cause bicultural bilinguals to change attitudes, feelings, and behaviors (along with language)—and not their language as such.

All this makes much less spectacular news, unworthy of a Reuters news story, but probably much closer to the truth.

Thinking and Dreaming in Bilinguals

One question bilinguals are often asked is, what language do they think in? I asked the same question in a small survey I conducted with bilinguals and trilinguals, and the answer was "both languages" (70 percent).[10] But before we try to understand this result, I should stress that thinking can often be independent of language. When people are walking down the street, riding a bus, or jogging in the woods, their thoughts may not be in a particular language, whether they are monolingual or bilingual. Philosophers and psychologists have long acknowledged that thought can be visual-spatial or involve nonlinguistic concepts. Some scholars, such as Steven Pinker and Jerry Fodor, propose that we have a "language of thought" (it has also been called "mentalese") that is prelinguistic; that is, it takes place before the representations we are thinking about are turned into French, English, or Spanish, for example. According to Pinker and Fodor (but there are opponents of this view), it is only at a later stage, in our planning to speak or subvocalizing, that individual languages actually intervene. It is then that we are sometimes conscious of the language that we have activated.

The "both languages" answer cited above is not surprising, since the bilinguals I asked probably took into account their "internal monologues" or "inner speech" when they answered. And since speech (in this case, nonverbalized speech) is normally used in different situations, with different people and for different purposes (see the discussion of the complementarity principle), their answer makes a lot of sense. Thus, were I to think about something I want to say in this book, after the "language of thought" (or mentalese) stage, it would be in English, because I am writing it in that language. Were I to think about a shopping list, it would be in French, as I live in a French-speaking region. Were I to think about what a friend told me the other day, it would be in the language that the friend used when we spoke. As linguist Aneta Pavlenko wrote to me, "In that way, context-specific activation . . . affects language selection for 'inner speech.'"[11]

Things are no different when one is dreaming. In the small survey I conducted, almost as many bilinguals and trilinguals (64 percent) said that they dreamed in one or the other language, depending on the dream (when they dreamed with language, of course). Once again, the complementarity principle is at work here: depending on the situation and the person we are dreaming about, we will use the one language, the other, or both. For example, a French-English bilingual in the United States once told me that he had dreamed about a little village in the French-speaking part of Switzerland that he knew well but to which he had not returned for several years. In his dream, he met an inhabitant of the village and he spoke French to him.

One interesting aspect of dreams in bilinguals is that some people have reported speaking a language fluently in a dream when they are not actually fluent in that language. The linguist Veroboj Vildomec reported that a multilingual who spoke some Russian dreamed that he was speaking fluent Russian. But when he woke up, he realized that it had been in fact a mixture of Czech and Slovak, with a bit of Russian, and not fluent Russian after all. Vildomec added that other bilinguals reported producing interferences during their dreams, that is, deviations in a language due to another language, even though they rarely made any when awake.[12]

It is true that some bilinguals are extremely careful to keep interferences out of their everyday speech, whereas when they are sleeping their brain can relax and let the other language seep in.

Emotions in Bilinguals

A particularly complex, and fascinating, aspect of bilingualism is how bilinguals deal with emotions in their languages:

> *Myth: Bilinguals express their emotions in their first language, which is usually the language of their parents.*

Despite this well-established (but erroneous) belief, things are not quite so simple. First, some bilinguals have grown up learning two languages simultaneously and hence have two first languages with which they will express their emotions. And for the majority of bilinguals who have acquired their languages successively—first one language and then, some years later, another—the pattern is not clear either. Aneta Pavlenko, who is herself multilingual, has spent many years researching the topic of emotions and bilingualism and has written a book on the subject, in which she concludes:

> I have tried to dismantle the myth of a simple, tangible, easily described relationship between the languages and emotions of bi- and multilingual speakers, and to show that this relationship plays out differently for different individuals, and even in the distinct language areas of a single speaker.[13]

This is not to say that some bilinguals do not prefer to express their emotions in their first, often their dominant, language. Think of all those bilinguals who have lived in the same place all their lives, who use their first language with their family and friends, who learned their second and third languages in adolescence, and who basically use the latter as work languages. It makes sense that they will express affect in their most-used language, that is, their first language. But as Pavlenko writes, it would be too simplistic to posit that late bilinguals have emotional ties only with their first language and have no such ties with their other languages.[14]

Some bilinguals who have had a traumatic experience in their first language, for example, may decide not to use it any longer when they are in a position to do so. Pavlenko cites Monika Schmid, a linguist who has worked a lot on language forgetting, who mentioned a married couple who had known each other in Germany just before the war, before emigrating. Because of the trauma of what they had lived through during the war, in more than fifty years of marriage they had never spoken German to each other, their first language, not even intimately.[15] There is also the case of the historian and author Gerda Lerner, who had joined the anti-Nazi resistance in Austria before emigrating in 1939 at age nineteen. Once settled in the United States, she refused to use her first language; she was repelled by it in every way. It was only some thirty years later that she reconciled herself with German.

Even without having lived through a traumatic experience, bilinguals may prefer using their second language over their first to convey emotions. One English-French bilingual, who had grown up in England and moved to France at age twenty-one, offered the following testimony:

> It is liberating to speak a language that is not one's
> mother tongue because it is easier to speak of taboo sub-
> jects . . . I find it easier to speak of anything connected

> with the emotions in French, whereas in an emotional
> situation in English I am rather tongue-tied, the affective
> content of the words is so much greater.

She explained to me that her English childhood had lacked affection and that it was in French that she had discovered what love meant. She ended her testimony with the words, "Perhaps one day I'll even manage to say [the English words], 'I love you.'" Another interesting testimony is given by the bilingual writer Nancy Huston. It concerns how she spoke to Léa, her baby girl, who was born some nine years after Huston had moved to Paris. She was going through a strong French-language period and had married a Bulgarian-French bilingual with whom she spoke French. Huston writes that she had started out using English baby talk with Léa but simply couldn't continue. The memories and the feelings that it stirred up were simply too strong for her to be able to continue in English. (Huston went through a very difficult time as a child when, at age six, she experienced her mother's abandonment of the family home.)[16]

Many late bilinguals mention that they can swear more easily in their second language. The same English-French bilingual quoted above wrote:

> I can ... swear much more easily in French and have a
> wider range of "vulgar" vocabulary ... I am finding that
> gradually the way I use French is influencing the way I
> use English—I can now say "shit" and "fuck off."

Huston, who wrote her master's thesis on linguistic taboo and swear words, analyzes this phenomenon, which she also experienced in her first years in Paris. She writes:

> The French language in general . . . was to me less
> emotion-fraught, and therefore less dangerous, than my
> mother tongue. It was cold, and I approached it coldly
> . . . This advantage, however, was not without its draw-
> backs. In a way, I was almost *too* free in French . . . I was
> untouched by the language. It did not talk to me, sing to
> me, rock me, slap me, shock me, scare me shitless. It was
> indifferent to me.[17]

When bilinguals are tired, angry, or excited, they naturally revert to the language in which they express their emotions, be it their first or their second language. Here is what a Portuguese-English bilingual told me:

> If there is something that makes me angry and if I allow
> some of my anger to come out, there is no doubt that I
> will use Portuguese, no matter the context or the situa-
> tion.

Pavlenko notes that sometimes when bilinguals are really angry, true communication is put aside and they may use a language that their spouse or child cannot understand. This can give them emotional satisfaction even if the words are not understood.[18]

Stress may cause interferences, problems in finding the appropriate word, and unintentional switching. Here is a personal experience. I was once bitten by a stingray while bathing in shallow waters in California. I was in real pain and bleeding quite badly. Since I was with a group of English-speaking people, I recall that I switched back and forth between English and French: I used the former language to ask them to take me to a doctor and I uttered French interjections to help express and ease the pain. In some very stressful situations, one language can even be completely cut off. Here is what an American Sign Language–English bilingual once wrote to me:

> One time I was in a very emotional situation and I was unable to speak, but the people with me could sign. They also were bilingual, so I signed and we communicated using sign language.

The language that is used in therapy is also very revealing. Paul Preston recounts how five of the American Sign Language–English bilinguals he interviewed said they felt blocked when in a therapy session because they could not express in English some of the things they really wanted to say in sign language.[19] And Nancy Huston states that she is convinced that she could not finish her own psychoanalysis because it was conducted in French, the language that made her feel protected at the time and the one in which her neuroses were under control.[20]

Emotions and bilingualism thus produce a very complicated and also very personal reality that has no set rules. Some bilinguals prefer to use one language, some the other, and some continue to use both of them. As Pavlenko writes, about her own habits:

> Each language . . . ties me differently, with bonds I cannot shake loose. And so, on a daily basis, I have no choice but to use both English and Russian when talking about emotions. "I love you," I whisper to my English-speaking partner. "Babulechka, ia tak skuchaiu po tebe [Grandma, I miss you so much]," I tenderly say on the phone to my Russian-speaking grandmother.[21]

12

Bilingual Writers

All groups of people have exceptional members, and it is with pleasure that I mention some of "our" exceptional people in the next two chapters. Few of us bilinguals will become like them (and we don't need to) but they are, in a linguistic sense, our Edmund Hillarys or Tenzing Norgays, and they have their place in our story.

In this chapter I will concentrate on bilingual writers, since writing is a specific area of language and probably one of the hardest cognitive skills that humans acquire. The language in which we learn to read and write fluently in our youth will normally remain the language we will use to write in for the rest of our lives. Of course, some people do write in another language, or several others, but they may not feel totally at ease doing so. However, in the small world of professional literary writing, one finds marked exceptions involving bilinguals. There are some bilingual authors who write books in their second (or third) language—an incredible feat when one thinks about how hard it is to write literature in one's own native language. And, even more exceptional, there are those who write literature in both of their languages. This chapter will be about these outstanding writers.

Writing in Your Second (or Third) Language

Many writers are bi- or multilingual, but they decide, despite this, to stick to one language for writing—usually their first language. Hence, Isaac B. Singer, for example, the Polish American writer and Nobel Prize winner, always wrote in his native language, Yiddish, even though he knew many other languages, notably Polish and Hebrew. Czesław Miłosz, also a Nobel laureate, was fluent in Polish, Russian, English, Lithuanian, and French, but wrote only in Polish.

A subgroup of these writers are those who choose to author their books in their most proficient writing language, even though it may not be their first language. Two examples come to mind. The first is Richard Rodriguez, the author of the best seller *Hunger of Memory,* whose very first language was Spanish but whose family switched over to English when he started going to school. Hence, English became his dominant language during his adolescence and definitely his writing language. The other example is Eva Hoffman, who moved to Canada from Poland when she was thirteen. She wrote her *Lost in Translation* in English, the language of her high school and university studies. Her book, like Rodriguez's, is a masterly account of her intellectual and human journey into mainstream American society and culture. Both authors have chosen to use English as their written language and have developed strong, sometimes unique, literary voices. Of course, as bilinguals themselves, they have the advantage of being able to oversee some of the translations that are done of their works, but they do not venture into literary creation in their less dominant language.

There are authors, however, who decide to write in their second or even their third language even though they have good writing proficiency in their first language. Probably the most famous is

Joseph Conrad, the early twentieth-century author of such classics as *Heart of Darkness, Lord Jim, Nostromo,* and *The Secret Agent.* Conrad was born Józef Teodor Konrad Korzeniowski in Poland, where he lived until the age of sixteen. He then lived in France for four years and became fluent in French. He joined the English merchant navy and learned to speak and write English. When he ended his sailing career at the age of thirty-five, he had already written some prose in English, and after that he became a full-time novelist. What is especially interesting is that he did not write his books in Polish, his first language, or in French, a language he wrote fluently, but in English, his *third* language.

According to Conrad's biographer Frederick Karl, his decision not to write in Polish was a way of separating himself from his father and his culture and country. Unfortunately, neither the British nor the Poles understood his situation; the British said that he was a Pole in disguise and the Poles said the reverse (a typical bicultural quandary). Conrad's English prose was superlative and required almost no editing, but in speaking he did retain a strong accent, which prevented him from lecturing publicly. Here, according to Karl, is what Conrad told a Belgian critic some twenty years after having settled down in England:

> My pronunciation [in English] is rather defective to this
> day. Having unluckily no ear, my accentuation is uncer-
> tain, especially when in the course of a conversation I be-
> come self-conscious. In writing I wrestle painfully with
> that language which I feel I do not possess but which
> possesses me—alas.[1]

Conrad retained complete fluency in Polish and French, and at home he would often carry on conversations in all three languages.

He also gave advice to translators who were translating his books into French and Polish.

Agota Kristof, a Hungarian-French bilingual, is a contemporary author who writes novels only in her second language. Kristof fled Hungary with her husband and their four-month-old baby during the 1956 uprising (she was twenty-one at the time) and came to settle down in Neuchâtel, Switzerland. She knew no other language than Hungarian when they first arrived, and she worked for a number of years in a local watchmaking factory. She then went back to school and studied French, thanks to a grant from the local university, and started on her literary career some twelve years after having moved to Switzerland. Her books, such as *The Notebook* (1986), a story of twin brothers lost in a country torn apart, have been translated into numerous languages. Her autobiography, *The Illiterate* (2004), recounts her forced emigration to Western Europe.[2]

Writing in Both Languages

As I have said, writing is a difficult skill, in whatever language, and writing literature is an art that only a handful of people ever master. And yet there is a group of exceptional bilinguals who write their works in two languages, not just one. I wish to examine those authors who went from writing in their first language to writing in their second language, those writers, even fewer, who started with their second language and then "moved back," as it were, to writing in their first, and authors who write bilingual works, using both languages in the same piece.

Some bilingual writers who immigrated at one or more points in their lives moved from writing in their first language to writing in their second or third language. Three such authors come to mind.

Vladimir Nabokov was born in St. Petersburg, Russia, in 1899 and was brought up trilingual in Russian, French, and English. At the age of twenty, he went to Cambridge, where he read French and Slavic literature. Nabokov became well known as an émigré writer in Russian, publishing such works as *Mashenka, The Gift,* and *The Eye* in that language. But later he wrote in English and became famous in the English-speaking world for such novels as *The Real Life of Sebastian Knight, Bend Sinister, Ada,* and *Lolita.* Nabokov also translated Russian works into English and English works into Russian (such as *Alice in Wonderland*).

The second author in this group is Samuel Beckett. Born in Ireland, a native speaker of English, he learned French at school and obtained a bachelor's degree in Romance languages and English. He never really used French in his daily life, however, until he became an instructor at the Ecole normale supérieure in Paris when he was twenty-two. His first works—tales and poems—were in English. In 1937, at the age of thirty-one, he moved to Paris permanently but continued to write in English; *Murphy,* for instance, was published in 1938. During World War II he took part in the Resistance in France and then went into hiding in the Vaucluse region. In 1951 his first French novel, *Molloy,* appeared, and from then on he wrote in both French and English. At that point, according to Elizabeth Beaujour, he stated that he didn't know in advance what language he would use for his next work.[3] Beckett received the Nobel Prize for Literature in 1969 for his contribution to the literature of two languages.

The third author is Elsa Triolet, born Elsa Kagan, a Russian French novelist of the twentieth century. She spent her early years in Russia and moved to France when she was twenty-two, after having met her first husband, André Triolet. Her early works were in Russian (*In Tahiti, Camouflage*). After divorcing Triolet, she married the French poet and novelist Louis Aragon, and the two had parallel literary careers. Her first book in French was *Good Evening, Theresa,* in 1938. It was followed by many other works, including *A Fine of Two Hundred Francs,* which was awarded the prestigious Prix Goncourt.

Elizabeth Beaujour has analyzed the reasons that led such authors to shift over to writing in their second (or third) language. One obvious reason is to be able to write for a wider audience. If you live in a country other than the one in whose language you are writing (you live in France and are writing in Russian, for example), you simply don't have that many readers for your works, even if the émigré community is quite large (as it happened to be for Nabokov and Triolet).

A second reason has to do with how the works are translated into the author's other language (Triolet's books in Russian, for example, were translated into French). Bilingual authors are rarely happy with the job that outside translators do with their work and they often edit the translations extensively. In the end, they frequently resort to translating their own works into their other language. But the process of self-translation turns out to be particularly tormenting for many (Beaujour talks of "the hell of self-translation"), and many bilingual authors express dissatisfaction with their own translations. Beaujour talks of Triolet's perception of the act of translating as the "terrifying spectre of noncoincidence with herself."[4] More recently, Ariel Dorfman wrote the following about his translation/adaptation of his book *Heading South, Looking North: A Bilingual Journey.*

> My rewriting of the memoir in Spanish after I completed
> it in English followed the structure, story, explorations of
> history and the mind which its rival language had set

out. Spanish had to overflow its words inside the house
that English built. And yet, how changed was that house
as it filled with Spanish. It was not the same book.[5]

A third reason that some bilingual writers move from writing
in their first to writing in their second language relates to the
complementarity principle: bilinguals use their languages for different purposes, in different domains of life, with different people.
Different aspects of life often require different languages. Beaujour
relates that Elsa Triolet realized that her Russian novel, *Camouflage,*
had been written in the "wrong" language, since it takes place in
France amid characters who speak, think, and feel French. Beaujour also tells us that when Nabokov Russianized his English best
seller *Lolita,* he had real problems finding appropriate terms for
descriptions dealing with cars, clothing, items of furniture, and
so on.[6]

Even though bilingual authors have good reasons for starting to
write in their second or third language, it is nonetheless difficult.
Triolet talks about the actual physical pain of writing her first book
in French (*Good Evening, Theresa*), and Nabokov says the same thing
in a more evocative way: he said it was like learning how to handle
things again after losing seven or eight fingers in an explosion![7]

As I stated at the beginning of this section, there is another
group of bilingual writers, a far smaller group, who start writing in
their second language and then revert to writing in their first language, something they had not done before. I had the pleasure of
meeting such a writer in Paris when I was preparing this book.
Nancy Huston was born in Canada and she lived there for a number of years before moving to the United States, where she went to
college. She left for Paris in 1973, where she did her master's thesis
with semiologist Roland Barthes. She stayed on in France, and

when she started to write, she decided to do so in her second language, French. Her first book, *Les Variations Goldberg*, came out in 1981 (*The Goldberg Variations* appeared in English many years later). She gives the following explanation for her decision to write in French:

> I suppose it was to do with the fact that my mother tongue was too emotionally fraught at the time. I preferred something more distant, more intellectual . . . I was in denial of my roots. No childhood, no mother, no problems. That worked for a number of years and then it stopped.[8]

Huston pursued her career as a French-language author for a number of years before deciding to write a novel in English, *Plainsong*, which came out some twelve years after her first book in French. She says of her return to English after her "first efforts" in French:

> My first efforts at fiction . . . tried to be savvy . . . I was starved for theoretical innocence. I longed to write long, free, wild, gorgeous sentences that explored all the registers of emotion, including—why not?—the pathetic. I wanted to tell stories wholeheartedly, fervently, passionately—and to *believe* in them, without dreading the derisive comments of the theoreticians.[9]

In a newspaper interview in 2008, she explained that French had become the language of exchange with her tax advisor and her children's teachers. Her return to English coincided with her return to the piano (from playing the harpsichord), "because," she said, "I'm strong enough to accept emotions."[10]

Nancy Huston now writes in both her languages and translates her works both ways. She states that translation is hard, tedious work, and that once she has finished translating a work, she suddenly feels that she could never have written the work in the other language![11] In 2005 Huston won the prestigious Prix Femina for *Ligne de faille,* which she had in fact first written in English *(Fault Lines)* and then translated into French.

While bilingual authors generally choose one language in which to write, writing in their first language only, or their second (or third), or alternating from one to the other, depending on the circumstance, a few decide to write bilingual works in which both languages are present on the same page (see Chapter 5 for a presentation of the bilingual language mode). Elizabeth Beaujour finds that in the twilight of their career, most bilingual writers are not satisfied keeping their two languages separate. They are in search of unity and wish their writing to exist in both languages. They can achieve this by making sure that all of their works are published in both languages (something that Beckett did, and Huston is currently doing), and they can have their characters act as bilinguals do, in a monolingual and also a bilingual way. Beaujour mentions Nabokov who, in *Ada,* had his characters speak three languages and shift from one language to another quite freely.[12]

Today, one does not need to be so advanced in one's literary career to write bilingually, as can be seen in the prose of two Hispanic American contemporary writers. Junot Díaz, a professor of writing at MIT and winner of the 2008 Pulitzer Prize for fiction for his book *The Brief Wondrous Life of Oscar Wao,* brings a lot of Spanish into his English prose (this particular code-switching style is often known as Spanglish). Here is a very short extract:

> [They] shrieked and called him gordo asqueroso! He forgot the perrito, forgot the pride he felt when the women in the family had called him hombre.[13]

Susana Chávez-Silverman is a Hispanic American author who has traveled in the Americas and holds a position at Pomona College in California. Her book *Killer Crónicas: Bilingual Memories* (2004) is based on the e-mails that she sent to colleagues and friends when she spent thirteen months in Buenos Aires. She too uses a blend of English and Spanish, but with a frequency of switches that is higher than normal, at least in the written mode. Here are a few lines from the beginning of one of her chapters:

> Como northern Califas girl, of course, había visto mucho
> nature espectacular; the Pacific Ocean como yarda de
> enfrente, for starters, y los sequoia giant redwoods. Yes,
> especially los redwoods. Pero también esa enredadera,
> don't know its name, the one with the huge, velvety deep
> purple blossoms y las fragile, hairy leaves and stems
> como patas de tarántula.[14]

Chávez-Silverman says that she remains bilingual in her writing so as to resist having to choose between the two languages; she hopes that her book will help establish a new trend for bilingual minority writing.

The list of bilingual writers working in their two languages, separately (usually) or together, is not long. As Elizabeth Beaujour says, the phenomenon remains rare:

> While it is not unusual for a writer to *be* a bilingual, it is
> still rare for a major modern writer to be bilingual or
> polyglot *as a writer* and to create a body of work of more
> or less equal weight in more than one language.[15]

As time goes by and bilingualism in all its aspects is more widely accepted, we may discover other writers, themselves bilingual, who never dared show their work in their other language (either the first or the second, or both), or who never managed to get it published. A fine example of one such writer is the much-acclaimed Jack Kerouac, the internationally known American novelist of the Beat generation. His *On the Road,* published in 1957 and translated into twenty-seven languages, remains a favorite among many for its anti-establishment, cross-country tale. What few people know is that Kerouac came from a French Canadian family established in Lowell, Massachusetts, and that he spoke French with his parents until the age of six; it was only then that he acquired English. Still fewer people realize that Kerouac wrote at least two books in French (the Quebec French variety known as joual): *La nuit est ma femme* and, discovered only in 2008, *Sur le chemin.* The latter (despite its title) is a different book from *On the Road* and was written shortly after the 1951 version of Kerouac's best seller. It was never published in French but Kerouac did translate it into English as *Old Bull in the Bowery.* Let us hope that many other *Sur le chemin*s, stored away in filing cabinets or in archives, will one day be published so that we can admire the bilingual creativity of their authors.

13

Special Bilinguals

This book is about regular, everyday bilinguals—that is, the great majority of those who lead their lives with two or more languages. There are, however, special bilinguals who have both a regular and sometimes also a unique relationship with their languages. In the previous chapter, we dealt with bilingual writers. Other special bilinguals, such as second-language teachers, and translators and interpreters, also make a living from their knowledge and use of their languages, while others may depend on their proficiency in their languages to do their job and to assure their safety (secret agents, for example). Among special bilinguals, we also find well-known people—known either because they are outstanding multilinguals or because they are famous for reasons that have nothing to do with their linguistic skills. These special people will be the subject of this chapter.

Second-Language Teachers

Teachers of second languages are also often called foreign-language teachers, although this can be a misnomer when the language they teach is used by millions of speakers in that country, such as Spanish in the United States or Arabic in France. There are two kinds of second-language teachers. First, there are those who teach the country's language, or languages, to others, mainly foreigners (for example, instructors of English as a second language who teach English to newly arrived immigrants in the United States). These teachers do not have to be bilingual in order to do their job and so we will not say much about them here.

Second, one finds teachers who teach a language other than the country's main language or languages. Examples would be teachers of German in England, teachers of English in Italy, and so on. They themselves form two groups. In the first group you find those who acquired the language they teach as a second language, in school or college. They may also have had a short stay in a country where the language they specialize in is used. This is the case with Ms. Wright, for example, who teaches Spanish at a high school in the Boston area. She took modern languages in college, studied Spanish and French, and then spent six months in Mexico. In the second group, you find native speakers of the language who have moved to another country and now teach their mother tongue. This is the case with Ms. Lopez, who teaches Spanish alongside Ms. Wright in the same school. She is originally Venezuelan and she moved to the United States as an adult after having gone to college in Caracas. She is a trained psychologist but took on language teaching when she arrived in the United States, after having followed a number of language-education courses at a local university.

Both Ms. Wright and Ms. Lopez teach Spanish to high school students of various levels. Based on the definition of bilingualism given in Chapter 2, the two are bilingual in that they use their two (or more) languages on a daily basis. Language teachers have varied fluency in the language they teach, and they may even have an accent in it, just like normal bilinguals, but they are special bilinguals in a number of ways. First, some, like Ms. Wright, do not use the language they teach outside the classroom very much, since they do not often have a need for it in everyday communication outside of work. Note, though, that this is not the case for Ms. Lopez, who has many Spanish-speaking friends and who uses both English and Spanish outside of school.

Second, they have insights into the linguistics of the language that normal language users do not have. For instance, how many speakers of English can explain, in a pedagogical way, the difference between the prepositions "for," "since," and "ago"? How many speakers of French can explain, in a clear manner, all the rules of the French past participle?

Third, second-language teachers are in a bilingual mode when teaching. When they are using the second language (for example, Spanish) overtly in class, they also have their other language (English here) available in case a student asks a question in it or code-switches for a word or expression. But they themselves may resort very rarely to code-switches and borrowings in front of students, and they may well correct those who slip into their better-known language.

Thus, in moments that would normally be conducive to code-switching and borrowing, and where the latter might facilitate communication, second-language teachers may refrain from calling upon the students' first language in order not to "set a bad example." Nevertheless, as users of the two languages themselves, and in private, they may code-switch and borrow. Having said this, I have also heard language teachers state that they refrain from code-switching outside school so as not to slip by accident into that behavior when they are teaching.

A fourth way in which such teachers are special bilinguals is that, even more so than regular bilinguals, they rarely believe they are bilingual, since many hold a very strict view of what it means to be bilingual (complete fluency in two or more languages, no accent in either language, and so on). When speaking to second-language teachers who feel this way, I often have to convince them that they are in fact bilingual, even though they clearly have special bilingual characteristics. Finally, they are usually true admirers of the second language they teach (most often in its standard variety) and they have a love for its culture, which they try to share with their students. Once again, this is often not the case with regular bilinguals, who concentrate less on their languages and cultures than on everyday aspects of life.

Translators and Interpreters

When we discussed the complementarity principle in Chapter 3, we saw that bilinguals are often not very good translators and interpreters. This is because, in domains covered by just one language, they do not always know the translation equivalents in the other language. Unless they acquired their second language explicitly, as in traditional second-language courses, bilinguals who are translating will find themselves lacking the vocabulary and also, at times, the linguistic skills and stylistic varieties needed to accomplish the translation. They may also lack the cultural knowledge attached to a language that would facilitate their understanding of the original text—a necessary step to be able to translate correctly.

Unlike regular bilinguals, translators and interpreters must have a complete set of translation equivalents in the other language. They must also know the two languages fluently (at all linguistic levels), and in addition they must have a good knowledge of the cultures concerned. Of course, the complementarity principle will continue to play a role, but it will be greatly reduced. Translators and interpreters, unlike regular bilinguals, have to learn to use their languages (and the underlying skills they have in them) for similar purposes and in similar domains of life. This is something regular bilinguals do not often need to do.

Translators indicate which language or languages they can translate *from* (these are their source languages) and which they can translate *into* (their target languages). For example, the source languages might be German and Spanish and the target language, English. In the translation and interpretation world, one speaks of active and passive languages. In the active-language category, language A is the person's native language or another language strictly equivalent to a native language (it is thus the target language). Language B is usually the first second language of which one has perfect command (it will usually also be a target language). In the passive-languages category, you find one or several languages for which the person has complete understanding; these will be the source languages. In addition, many translators and interpreters specialize in domains, such as law, finance, or politics.

Translation is a special bilingual skill: you try to express in one language, in as faithful a way as possible, the meaning and the style of a text in another language. This means fully understanding the original text in the source language, and having the necessary transfer skills, as well as the linguistic and cultural skills, in the target language. Very little room is left for the translator's own intuition or creativity. He or she must follow the original text as exactly as possible and render it in correct prose in the target language. It is no wonder, then, that there are specialized schools where students learn the skills linked to translation, usually at the master's-degree level (for example, the Monterey Institute of International Studies in California, and the Ecole de traduction et d'interprétation in Geneva). One of the requirements for entry is to have excellent language skills in two or more languages. Training then transforms the student into a certified translator.

There are literally hundreds of thousands of translators in the world today, many working in the shadow of international institutions, government bodies, large corporations, publishing companies, and so on. As in every other trade, there are certain "champions," translators esteemed for their skills who are unknown to the public but who are well known and highly respected by their peers. There are also some renowned authors who were (or are) translators. For instance, the French poet Charles Baudelaire produced an immensely successful translation of the works of Edgar Allan Poe; the Russian American author Vladimir Nabokov translated *Alice in Wonderland* into Russian, as well as works (often poetry) by Verlaine, Tennyson, Byron, Keats, Shakespeare, and so on; and the Argentinean writer Jorge Luis Borges translated many English, French, and German works into Spanish.

Simultaneous interpreters have an even more complex set of skills. In addition to what has been described for translators, one must add all the linguistic and cognitive skills that allow interpreters to go from hearing oral input in one language to producing oral output in the other language, either simultaneously or successively.[1] This involves, among other things, careful listening, processing and comprehending the input in the source language, memorizing it, formulating the translation in the target language, and then articulating it, not to mention dual tasking (letting the next sequence come in as you are outputting the preceding one), note taking in some types of interpretation, and careful enunciation. Interpreter training is therefore very demanding and requires additional years of study.

In terms of language mode, interpreters work in a bilingual mode, but one language is not more active than the other, as in regular bilinguals' communication. Both languages (the source language and the target language) have to be active to the same extent. The interpreter has to be able to hear the input (source) language and also the output (target) language, not only for self-monitoring of what she is interpreting but also in case the speaker uses the target language in the form of code-switches. However, the source-language production mechanisms must be tightly shut off (deactivated) so that the interpreter does not slip into simply repeating what she is hearing instead of interpreting it (as sometimes happens when interpreters get very tired). Given all of these requirements, it is no wonder that interpreters, like translators, are considered special bilinguals, and that regular bilinguals are not born translators and interpreters. A bilingual student learned this the hard way when he tried out for a position as an interpreter:

> When I was a student in Paris, I found an ad one day
> stating that interpreters were being sought for a one-day
> conference. They would be interpreting from English into
> French. Naive as I was—aren't all bilinguals born inter-
> preters, I told myself—I went to the office that was orga-
> nizing the conference. They were very welcoming and I
> felt quite confident I could get the job. I was put into a
> booth for a trial run and I put on the headphones
> handed to me. The first sentence came through and I
> managed to interpret it quite nicely. This is going to be a

breeze, I told myself. But problems started immediately. As I was outputting the first sentence, the second one was already coming in and I wasn't paying enough attention to it. I could remember its beginning but not its ending. I struggled on but very quickly fell behind the recorded voice and I just couldn't say anything more after a few minutes. I left the booth, and the office, not very proud of myself. The scene remains vivid in my mind some forty years later and since then I have had the utmost respect for interpreters and the training they have to go through to do their job well.[2]

Secret Agents

Many of us believe that agents who work for intelligence services are probably bilingual and bicultural, in the image of Jack Higgins's Kurt Steiner in *The Eagle Has Landed,* a novel about a German attempt to kidnap Winston Churchill during World War II. In the story, Steiner's father was a major general in the German army and his mother was American. Steiner himself, the leader of a German commando unit, had been brought up in both England and Germany and was perfectly bilingual.

As I was researching the literature to find out about the bilingualism of secret agents, I realized that there was very little written about their linguistic skills. And as I dug further, I slowly understood that the classic view we all have is not quite as clear-cut as it would seem. Not all agents, for example, need to know another language well, so long as they are in contact with someone who is bilingual. Thus, a spy who passes government secrets to a member of a foreign embassy can do so in her native language if the embassy member (perhaps an attaché of some kind) acts as a bilingual go-between. This is true also for agents who agree to work for a foreign power while staying put in their home country and gradually moving up within various government structures. This was the case with the Cambridge Five in England, notably Kim Philby and Guy Burgess, who spied for the Soviet Union in the middle of the last century while occupying important positions in the British establishment.

"Sleeper" or deep-cover agents are placed by the spying power in a target country and are often natives of that country (or nationals of both countries). Just recently, an example of a sleeper agent received a lot of press. George Koval was born in 1913 in Sioux City, Iowa, and he grew up there as a normal American boy. He played baseball and, of course, spoke fluent American English. During the Depression, his parents and he emigrated to a Siberian city in a region that Stalin had proposed as a Jewish homeland. His parents were committed to communism, and Koval was strongly influenced by them. He was trained at the Institute of Chemical Technology in Moscow and was recruited by the GRU (the largest Russian intelligence agency). Koval was then sent back to the United States and for a number of years was inactive as an agent (his code name was Delmar). He was drafted into the U.S. Army and, little by little, his duties brought him into contact with the atomic bomb project (notably, aspects dealing with the fuel used). What he learned was extremely valuable for the development of the Russian bomb, which was detonated for the first time in 1949. Koval was a very successful agent not only because he was intelligent and well trained (this gave him access to the heart of the bomb project) but also because he was a "genuine" American. He spoke fluent English, he loved baseball, and he was just a regular guy. He fled back to the Soviet Union after the war, when he realized that U.S. counterintelligence was closing in on him.

Agents like Koval, though, who in some ways coincide with what we imagine them to be—that is, perfectly bilingual and bicultural—do not represent the majority of agents. Let me conclude this discussion with the example of Britain's Special Operations Executive (SOE) agents, who operated during World War II. The task of the SOE was to infiltrate agents into occupied Europe so that they could organize, inspire, and assist the local resistance groups fighting the Nazi presence. They were taught how to use guns and explosives, transmit messages, carry out acts of sabotage, defend themselves, and so on, and they were either parachuted into the area they were to work in or flown in using light airplanes. Those recruited were either nationals of the country in question or knew it very well. Many of the latter had at least one parent from the target country, or they had worked or gone to school there before the war. For example, one SOE agent in France, Gilbert Norman, was the son of an English father and a French mother and he had been educated in both countries. Another agent, Jack Agazarian, had an Armenian father and a French mother, and had gone to schools in both France and England.

However, other SOE agents were far from being proficient bilinguals. For example, a very successful agent in the Besançon region of France, George Millar (his alias was Emile) spoke good French—but with a strong Scottish accent! He writes in his memoir that he could pass as a Frenchman in front of any German, but he knew that a real Frenchman would know right away that he wasn't French. Since the Germans were often aided by the French Vichy police in their hunt for Resistance fighters, this was potentially a problem. In fact, one day Millar was stopped by two French police officers, who asked him who he really was. He had to admit that he was British and, much to his surprise, they let him go, as they were friendly with the Resistance.[3] Unfortunately, other SOE agents were not as lucky as Millar. Francis Suttill, the head of a "circuit" (Resistance network) in the Paris region, had a very poor accent in French, despite having a French mother. To make sure he was understood, he had to rely on the help of a "courier," a young French SOE agent, Andrée Borrel. In addition to the problem of Suttill's strong accent, apparently some of Suttill's agents would get together in black-market restaurants and would talk things over—in English.[4]

Suttill's circuit (named Prosper) was penetrated by the Germans and many agents were caught and imprisoned. After they had been interrogated, they were sent to concentration camps in Germany. Unfortunately, very few managed to survive the ordeal. The reasons for the Prosper disaster are many (one being that there was a traitor among the SOE agents) and a lack of linguistic skills probably does not rank among them. But had the bilingualism and biculturalism of the British agents been total—something one does not expect in regular bilinguals—and had some of them been more careful with their language behavior in public, their chances of remaining free would probably have been better. Nevertheless, these agents were extremely devoted and courageous, and one can only have gratitude for what they undertook in very difficult circumstances. They sacrificed their lives so that France and Europe could be free of the German occupation.

Well-Known Bilinguals

I will end with a few special bilinguals or multilinguals who are well-known people. In the first category are individuals who are outstanding learners and speakers of many languages. They are often called polyglots or even linguists (in the sense of being multi-lingual). Such people are talked about with wonder by monolinguals who go through life with just one language, and by regular bilinguals who may know "only" three or four languages to varying degrees, as is my case. One such person who is often mentioned is Cardinal Giuseppe Mezzofanti, who lived astride the eighteenth and nineteenth centuries and was reported to speak fluently some fifty to sixty languages. Another polyglot often evoked is the British explorer, ethnologist, and diplomat Sir Richard Francis Burton, who lived in the nineteenth century. He is reported to have acquired four languages in his youth and then some twenty-five others as an adult, including Gujarati, Marathi, Hindustani, Persian, and Arabic, not to mention many dialects. Burton lived in India, among other places, and explored the Arabian Peninsula and the upper Nile region, and hence made good use of the languages that he acquired.

Professional linguists who study languages as well as language structure and language processing usually know just a few languages, but some are true polyglots. For example, Mario Pei, an Italian American linguist in the past century, and a best-selling author in his field, was reported to be able to speak some forty languages and to be acquainted with the linguistics of about a hundred languages. Another linguist, the late Ken Hale, who taught at MIT, specialized in endangered indigenous languages, which he also learned with great ease. Among his languages we find Navajo, Jemez, Hopi, Tohono O'odham, Warlpiri, and Ulwa.

Leaving aside these rare people, there are many bilinguals who are well known not because they master or mastered a large number of languages, but because of their various other activities. Bilingualism is (or was) just part of their everyday life. In the domain of philosophy and religion, for example, Erasmus, the famous Dutch humanist, spoke five languages, partly owing to the fact that he lived in several countries, notably England, France, and Switzerland. He used Latin not only for diplomacy and theology but also in everyday conversations. Pope John Paul II was reported to speak twelve languages, some of which he probably used daily, such as Polish, Latin, Italian, and English. As for his successor, Pope Benedict XVI, in addition to being able to read Ancient Greek and biblical Hebrew, he speaks German fluently as well as Italian, French, English, and Latin. The most surprising bilingual in this category is Jesus Christ, who may have been tri- or quadrilingual. His mother tongue was Aramaic; he then learned Hebrew in his rabbinical training and he may also have known Greek and Latin, both of which were spoken in Palestine at the time.

In the domain of politics and diplomacy, one of the founding fathers of the United States, Benjamin Franklin, who was also a diplomat, scientist, inventor, and printer, was reported to be fluent in six languages (English, French, Italian, Spanish, Latin, and German). Closer to our time, former Canadian prime minister Pierre Trudeau was a French-English bilingual, Prime Minister Indira Gandhi of India knew at least two languages (Hindi and English), and President Tito of Yugoslavia was fluent in five languages. The current governor general of Canada, Michaëlle Jean, is fluent in French, English, Haitian Creole, Spanish, and Italian. Former U.S. secretary of state Henry Kissinger is a German-English bilingual, and is easily recognized by his deep voice and rather strong German accent. Madeleine Albright, who occupied the same position, was born in Prague and is fluent in Czech, Russian, English, and French; she also has reading abilities in several other languages. Associate Justice of the U.S. Supreme Court Sonia Sotomayor is bilingual in Spanish and English, as is Hilda Solis, secretary of labor in the Obama administration. Daniel Cohn-Bendit, the charismatic leader of the May 1968 events in France and currently a member of the European Parliament, is totally bilingual in French and German. He appears on talk shows in both Germany and France and goes back and forth between his two languages, which he speaks with no accent. At least two members of French president Nicolas Sarkozy's first cabinet, Rachida Dati and Fadéla Amara, are bilingual in Arabic and French, although one rarely hears them speak their first language, which is a minority language in France.

Many famous scientists were (or are) bilingual, often because of immigration. Here are just a few, along with their main languages: Albert Einstein (German, English), Sigmund Freud (German, English), Marie Curie (Polish, Russian, French), Guglielmo Marconi (Italian, English), Bruno Bettelheim (German, English), and Roman Jakobson (Russian, French, English, German, and Czech).

In the domain of classical music and fine arts, George Frideric Handel, the Baroque composer, was a German-Italian-English trilingual. The composer and piano virtuoso Frédéric Chopin had a French father and hence spoke fluent French as well as Polish. Arthur Rubinstein spoke Polish, the language of the country he was born in, as well as German, French, and English. Yo-Yo Ma, cellist and composer, speaks Chinese and English. As for artists, Vincent van Gogh was bilingual in Dutch and French, Pablo Picasso was at least bilingual in Spanish and French, and Marc Chagall was trilingual (Russian, English, and French).

The media are increasingly international, and many journalists and reporters are bi- or multilingual. Here are just a few well-known examples: Christiane Amanpour (English, Farsi, French), Ralitsa Vassileva (English, Bulgarian), Octavia Nasr (Arabic, English, French), María Elena Salinas (Spanish, English), Olivier Todd (French, English), Nelson Monfort (French, Spanish, English, and Italian), and Jonathan Mann (English, French).

In the field of show business, many bilingual singers, such as Shakira, Nana Mouskouri, Céline Dion, Gloria Estefan, Christina Aguilera, Lhasa de Sela, and Julio Iglesias, sing in at least two languages, sometimes many more. As for actors and comedians, many are bilingual, such as Eva Longoria Parker and Andy García (both Spanish-English bilinguals), Aziz Ansari (English, Tamil), Margaret Cho (Korean, English), and Maz Jobrani (English, Farsi). Some actors actually have taken roles in the other language or languages they know and use, for example Jodie Foster (English, French), Sophia Loren (Italian, French, English), Charlotte Gainsbourg (French, English), and Lambert Wilson (French, English). In fact, in certain countries with a large minority language population (such as the Hispanic population in the United States), there is now a demand for bilingual actors.

Finally, the domain of sports is simply replete with bilinguals. I'll mention just a few and let the reader add other names and other sports: tennis (Roger Federer, Rafael Nadal), baseball (numerous major-league players from Cuba, the Dominican Republic, Japan, Mexico, and elsewhere), motor sports (Fernando Alonso, Kimi Räikkönen, Felipe Massa), soccer (Thierry Henry, Patrick Vieira, Jens Lehmann), basketball (Yao Ming, Tony Parker), and so on.

II

Bilingual Children

14

In and Out of Bilingualism

As adult speakers, we never fail to be amazed by children who speak a second or a third language. Some four-year-old little girl will tell you something in English and then switch over to Spanish to answer her mother's question, or a twelve-year-old boy will offer to translate into French what his German friend is saying. How do they do it? we ask ourselves. The next six chapters will offer some answers to this question. In this chapter, I examine cases of children who become bilingual at different moments in their childhood; I also discuss bilingual children who revert to monolingualism. We will then examine the reasons that underlie this to-and-fro movement—into bilingualism, as well as out of bilingualism.

Becoming Bilingual

Children who acquire two languages from the very start (that is, simultaneously) continue to intrigue researchers, but they are in fact far rarer than children who acquire one language and then another (we will study both cases in the next chapter). To acquire two languages together, the family usually adopts an approach by which the child receives two language inputs (perhaps one language is spoken by the mother, the other by the father, or one language by the parents and the other by a caretaker such as a nanny or a day-care center). Let me give two examples. Hildegard, an American little girl, acquired two languages simultaneously, since her father spoke German to her and her mother spoke English. Between the ages of two and five, she was dominant in English because the family lived in an English-speaking environment. She was a lively little girl, quickly aware of the two languages, and she tried out various ways of getting her father to also speak English, such as by asking him, "How does Mama say it?" Her German became less fluent as time went by but it got a real boost when Hildegard spent a bit more than half a year in Germany during her fifth year. In fact, as is often the case, after only four weeks in a totally German environment, she was unable to produce more than a few very simple utterances in English. Of course, when she returned to the United States, she quickly recovered her English, and after four weeks it was her German that was starting to weaken. Then things settled down, and Hildegard continued her journey in bilingualism with no problems.

Hildegard's story is similar to that of many children who acquire their languages simultaneously: one language weakens if the environment favors the other, there are very rapid shifts in dominance if the main language changes, and there are even signs that a language is forgotten for a while, although it can be revived quickly if conditions are right. As it happens, Hildegard's story is also a classic in the field of bilingualism, as her father, Werner Leopold, published one of the first exhaustive case studies on the simultaneous acquisition of two languages.[1] It is based on Hildegard, who is probably the most studied bilingual child in linguistic history.

If the second language does not come from one of the parents, it can come from other caretakers, as my second example shows. Suzanne, who now lives in the United States, told me that when she was an infant in Africa, her nanny spoke Swahili to her. Suzanne was fluent in that language until age seven, in addition to the French she spoke with her parents. The family then moved to a Portuguese-speaking country and her Swahili was replaced by Portuguese. She continues her story below; as the reader will see, juggling languages did not scare this family:

> French was spoken at home, English at school, and Portuguese at home and in the community. With my older sister I always tended to use English, whereas with my younger sister I spoke Portuguese. My two sisters would communicate mostly in Portuguese, but the three of us always spoke French with our parents.[2]

If there are several caretakers and people who matter in the life of the young child, and if they use different languages, then it is not uncommon that the child will pick them all up. Here is the testimony of a person who lived in India at the turn of the twentieth century and who noticed that very young English children acquired several Indian languages so as to be able to speak with people who were in their immediate proximity. They also sometimes acted as interpreters for their parents:

> It is a common experience in the district of Bengal [India] in which the writer resided to hear English children three or four years old who have been born in the country conversing freely at different times with their parents in English, with their *ayahs* [nurses] in Bengali, with the

[groundsmen] in Santali, and with the house servants in Hindustani.[3]

An important moment in the early life of children who become bilingual is when they start going to school and begin to socialize with other children. If the school or the environmental language is different from what they speak at home, then they will acquire it, sometimes easily and sometimes with more difficulty (see Chapter 19 for a discussion of bilingualism and education). For example, anthropologist Carroll Barber, who studied Yaqui Indians in Arizona, tells us that their children, whose first language is Yaqui, acquire their second and third languages at about age five or six: Spanish through contact with Mexican American children in and out of school, and English in school, where it is the medium of instruction.[4] Similarly, young Tanzanian children acquire at least three languages: the local language in the home and immediate surroundings, Swahili in the community and at school, and English at school.[5] If the school system itself starts with one language as the medium of instruction and then moves on to another, several languages can be involved. Marie-Paule Maurer tells us about Létitia, a young girl of Portuguese origin in Luxembourg. Her first language was Portuguese, but when she went to kindergarten she acquired Luxembourgish, a German dialect. The school language then switched over to standard German in first grade. French came in as a "second" language in second grade, and little Létitia also had Portuguese lessons she attended twice a week.[6] Given this example, it is no wonder that the people in Luxembourg are among the most multilingual in the world!

As children grow older, different events in their lives can lead them to acquire a second, third, or fourth language. Immigration is one of those important events. Quite literally millions of immigrants to North America and to Europe have been confronted with the language of a new country in their childhood and adolescence. Eva Hoffman, the author of *Lost in Translation,* recalls vividly her first day in a Canadian school at age thirteen, accompanied by her sister:

> "Shut up, shuddup," the children around us are shouting, and it's the first word in English that I understand from its dramatic context. My sister and I stand in the schoolyard clutching each other, while kids all around us are running about, pummelling each other, and screaming like whirling dervishes.[7]

Despite her ordeal of changing countries as well as languages, schools, and even her first name, to integrate her more quickly, Eva Hoffman succeeded brilliantly in her studies and in her career. Unfortunately, not all children who are put in such a "sink or swim" context make it through as well as Eva.

Without actually immigrating, many children and adolescents spend time in another region or in another country in order to acquire the language there. This has happened throughout human history—as far back as ancient Rome, when Roman families would send their children to Greece to be educated and to learn Greek. In the country I now live in, Switzerland, there is a long-standing tradition of spending time during one's adolescence in another part of the country so as to pick up the language more easily (for example, many Swiss German teenagers spend a year, sometimes less, as au pairs or apprentices in the French-speaking part of the country).

Reverting to Monolingualism

One often hears about, or reads about, children becoming bilingual, sometimes in a very short time span, and one marvels at how they do it. One rarely hears the same types of stories about children who revert back to monolingualism after having been bilingual. And yet they are just as much a part of our story, even though people cherish language acquisition more than language forgetting. Let me mention two cases. The first one concerns Stephen, the sixteen-month-old child of anthropologist Robbins Burling, who accompanied his parents to the Garo Hills district of Assam in India. Stephen began using Garo words within a few weeks of their arrival, although his English remained dominant at first. Since he had a Garo nurse, his Garo improved quickly, in particular when his mother was hospitalized and he was left mainly in the care of his nurse. In addition, his father often spoke Garo to him. The family traveled to another region of India a bit later on and his English picked up again, especially because his mother was back. When the family left the Garo region, Stephen, who was a bit more than three, was truly bilingual in Garo and English, maybe with a slight dominance in Garo. He translated and switched from one language to the other as bilingual children do.[8]

Robbins Burling's account is particularly interesting, as he takes time to tell us about Stephen's return to monolingualism. When the family traveled across India, Stephen would try to speak Garo with Indians he met, but he soon realized that they did not speak it (Garo is spoken only by a bit more than half a million inhabitants). The last time he tried to use the language was in the plane going back to the United States. He thought that the Malayan boy sitting next to him was a Garo and, as Burling writes, "A torrent of Garo tumbled forth as if all the pent-up speech of those weeks had been suddenly let loose." His father did try to speak Garo to Stephen when they were back in the States, but after a few months he did not respond to his father's Garo. Burling did not know if it was a lack of understanding or a refusal to speak the "wrong" language. Within six months of their departure from the Garo Hills, Stephen was having problems with the simplest of Garo words. Robbins Burling finishes his report in the following way:

> At the age of five and a half, Stephen is attending kinder-garten in the United States. He speaks English perhaps a bit more fluently and certainly more continuously than most of his contemporaries. The only Garo words he now uses are the few that have become family property, but I hope that some day it will be possible to take him back to the Garo Hills and to discover whether hidden deep in his unconscious he may not still retain a remnant of his former fluency in Garo that might be reawakened if he again came in contact with the language.[9]

The intriguing point that Burling raises concerns whether one can recover a language acquired in very early childhood, and also forgotten very early on. It is reported that the forgotten language sounds familiar and that certain sounds are not difficult to pronounce, but no real studies have managed to give us clear information on how much is retained and how quickly the language can be relearned. All of us who have a childhood language deep inside our minds have a hidden wish that we will one day be able to reactivate it and use it in everyday life. As for Stephen, Robbins Burling told me via e-mail that Stephen never did go back to the Garo Hills. However, when he was six he acquired Burmese in Rangoon (now

Yangon). He spoke it quite fluently for a year but then forgot it. As his father wrote to me, by age eight Stephen had learned three languages and forgotten two![10]

The second example of a child who reverted to monolingualism is closer to us, geographically and temporally. This case study, related by linguist Lily Wong Fillmore, concerns Kai Fong, the son of a Chinese (Cantonese) immigrant family, who arrived in the United States when he was five. He was raised mainly by his Chinese grandmother, as the parents spent long hours in their San Francisco-area restaurant. When he started going to school, Kai Fong had difficulties: he was teased by the other boys because of his clothes and his haircut. After a rock-throwing incident he was involved in, and the reprimand that followed, he started becoming more withdrawn both at school and at home. He went through a period when he knew both Cantonese and English, but quite quickly he switched to speaking English to his grandmother, who could not understand him. By age ten, he was spending more time outside the home, with English-speaking friends, and he no longer seemed to understand Cantonese well. Among his three siblings, only one, a sister, still communicated in Cantonese with the parents and the grandmother. All the adults were disconcerted by this rapid loss of the family language. Wong Fillmore ends her report as follows:

> The shift from Cantonese to English in this family and
> the loss of the family language by the children have had a
> great impact on communication between the adults and
> the children and ultimately on family relations. There is
> tension in this home: The adults do not understand the
> children, and the children do not understand the adults.
> Father, Mother, and Grandmother do not feel they know

the children, and they do not know what is happening in their lives.[11]

Fortunately, not all cases of language forgetting are as difficult as this one. Normally, parents learn enough of the majority language to interact, to some extent at least, with their children who speak it exclusively. In this particular case, the grandmother never learned English and the parents spoke it very badly, particularly the mother. As for Kai Fong, who went from being monolingual in Cantonese, to being bilingual in Cantonese and English, to being monolingual in English, all in the span of a few years, I asked Lily Wong Fillmore how he was doing. She replied that he was twenty-three or twenty-four years old now (this was in 2008) and added, "I hope he is more comfortable with who he is."

An Explanation

We have seen how children can go in and out of bilingualism in a very short time. Figure 14.1 outlines the factors that underlie this phenomenon. In the figure, the main factor leading to the development of a language is the *need* for that language (language X in the figure). The need can be of various sorts: to communicate with family members, caretakers, friends, some or all of whom may be monolingual in that language; to participate in the activities of a day care or a school; to interact with people in the community. The need can also be, quite simply, to watch television, do sports, and so on. In a word, the child has to feel that he or she really needs a particular language. If that is so, and other factors are favorable, then the child will develop the language. If the need disappears or isn't really there (perhaps the parents also speak the other language but

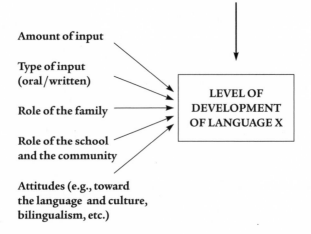

Figure 14.1. Factors leading to the acquisition and maintenance of another language in children.

pretend they don't), and other factors are unfavorable, then the child will no longer use the language and there is a fair chance that it will be forgotten.

Let me go back to the example concerning Hildegard to see how it fits in with the need factor. She needed to communicate with each of her parents and hence acquired two languages, even though English became dominant because she lived in the United States. But when she went to Germany, she needed German more and her dominance shifted. On her return to the United States, she reverted to being dominant in English.

How about language forgetting? Clearly Stephen felt he no longer needed Garo when he left India. He knew that his father, the only other Garo speaker in the family, also spoke English, and he didn't feel, unconsciously of course, that he needed to keep it up just to please him. Children don't like pretending when it comes to something as vital as the language used with a parent. As for Kai Fong, after a difficult beginning at school, he needed to fit in in his new country, and he found more solace with his English-speaking friends than he did at home, and so he let go of his Cantonese, even though it meant not being able to communicate with some of his family. The need for English was simply far greater than that for Cantonese.

In Figure 14.1, the other factors that play a role in the level of development of a language are listed on the left. Let me go through them and give some examples. First, children require a certain amount of input of the language in order to acquire it. Annick De Houwer, a well-known specialist on childhood bilingualism, stresses the fact that for children to "pick up" a language, they need to have language input in a variety of situations from people who matter to them—parents, caretakers, members of the extended family, friends, and so on.[12] Second, the type of input that children receive is important. Bilingual speech containing code-switches and borrowings is bound to occur in the family, but if one can find ways of giving children moments of "monolingual" input, as naturally as possible, then it is all for the better. Sometimes the monolingual role can be taken on by members of the extended family who do not know the other language or by monolingual caretakers (for example in day care or kindergarten). Another type of input is written language. Annick De Houwer stresses the importance of reading to children, as it is an excellent source of vocabulary and cultural information that they may not have in their normal environment. Later, if the child becomes literate in the language, then moments dedicated to personal reading will be important.[13]

A third factor is the role of the family. We will return to this aspect in a later chapter, so it is enough to say here that, if at all possible, parents and caretakers should be aware of what their children are going through as they are acquiring (or losing) a language. They should adopt family strategies to reinforce the home language if it is the minority language and if it is in danger of being replaced by the majority language spoken outside the home. Input from extended family members and friends who use the language is precious and shows children that using that language is quite natural.

The role of the school and the larger community is also crucial for the child's development of a language. Although we will deal with bilingualism and education in another chapter, I should stress here how important schools and communities are in the acquisition of a language, or in its loss. If the minority language is not given support in the school or in the community, there is a good chance that it will lessen in importance, if not simply be put aside, especially if the majority language is present in every aspect of the child's life. Here is the testimony of a young French couple concerning their son, who lost his French not even a year after they moved to the United States:

> When we first arrived . . . Cyril, our eldest and then only
> son was almost two and was making fine progress in

learning French. For some time after our arrival, French
remained the only language of interaction in the home,
but English did start making inroads, through American
friends and through children's television programs . . .
Cyril started to attend day care and hence began to learn
English, and it wasn't long before he began speaking it
along with French at home. We would, of course, only
speak to him in French and insist that he answer back in
French, but enforcing this became difficult when friends
of his would come home to play. In addition, speaking
one language and being answered back in the other became tiring, and little by little we started answering back
in English. With time, Cyril used less and less French
with us, and he slowly became monolingual in English.[14]

The final factor proposed in the figure concerns the attitudes
people have toward the language and culture that need support,
as well as toward bilingualism. Children are extremely receptive
to the attitudes of their parents, teachers, and peers. Here is what
one person told me about the negative bias French-speaking Bel-
gians have toward Flemish, a language that is taught in French-
speaking schools but that children simply don't seem to be able to
learn well:

> Our early education is often biased by the fact that our
> parents transmit prejudices about the other group.
> Therefore it is sometimes hard to find the motivation for
> learning the other language. [In addition] French-
> speaking people . . . are very unwilling to learn Flemish,
> as the only places where they could use it are Belgium
> and Holland.[15]

Clearly, negative attitudes about a language and its culture and the lack of need for the language, at least when one is young, do not augur well for the child's acquisition of that language.

As for attitudes toward bilingualism, one is surprised by how little people know about it, and by the preconceived ideas they have concerning what it means. I have presented some of these myths and discussed them throughout the book. People also have preset beliefs about children and bilingualism. The following is one such idea:

> *Myth: The language spoken in the home will have a negative effect on the acquisition of the school language, when the latter is different.*

This is totally wrong. On the contrary, the home language can be used as a linguistic base for acquiring aspects of the other language. It also gives children a known language to communicate in (with parents, caretakers, and, perhaps, teachers) while acquiring the other. In his book *Hunger of Memory,* Richard Rodriguez relates how nuns from his Catholic school came to his home to ask his parents to stop using Spanish with him. This kind of thing happens often because professionals, many with good intentions, tender advice concerning bilingualism that is not always based on scientific facts. Richard Rodriguez's parents complied and he never fully developed his Spanish when he could have been fluent in both his languages, in speech and writing. His parents, like many other parents who "let go of the home language," then had to explain to family members why their children could no longer speak it.

> Embarrassed, my parents would regularly need to explain
> their children's inability to speak flowing Spanish during
> those years. My mother met the wrath of her brother, her

only brother, when he came up from Mexico one summer
with his family. He saw his nieces and nephews for the
very first time. After listening to me, he looked away and
said what a disgrace it was that I couldn't speak Spanish,
"*su proprio idioma.*"[16]

It is crucial that parents, and also professionals who are involved
with bilingual children, learn about bilingualism. It will allow them
to understand what the children are going through, and help them
offer the support that bilingual children need.

15

Acquiring Two Languages

As we know, children become bilingual either by acquiring two languages at the same time (simultaneously) or by acquiring them one after the other (successively). Linguists diverge over the age that separates the two types of acquisition, but most would agree that up to age four, children are in a simultaneous acquisition mode whereas as from age five on they are in a successive mode. Whatever the type of acquisition, the degree of bilingualism attained can be the same. The factors that we examined in the previous chapter condition the extent of a child's bilingualism and how long the child will be bilingual, but not the type of acquisition.

Simultaneous Bilingualism

In this type of bilingualism, children acquire two languages (sometimes even three) at the same time, from the very beginning of language onset. Simultaneous bilinguals are far less numerous than children who acquire their two languages successively (certainly less than 20 percent of bilingual children).[1] Simultaneous bilingualism occurs when each parent uses a different language with their child (for example, the father uses Spanish and the mother English) or the parents use one language and other caretakers (a member of the family, a nanny, the personnel in the child's day care) use another language. Hence the child receives a dual language input and, over the first years, acquires two languages.

A topic that worries many parents is the rate of language acquisition, since some people hold the following view:

Myth: Bilingualism will delay language acquisition in children.

Although there is some variability in the rate of language acquisition among bilingual children, as there is among monolingual children, the main milestones are reached within the same age spans in the two groups. Let me take a few examples, starting with the very first stage, babbling. Psycholinguist D. Kimbrough Oller and his colleagues compared the development of canonical babbling (that is, babbling using well-formed syllables, such as "da da da") in monolingual and bilingual infants and found that the two groups started babbling at the same age.[2] As concerns the capacity to perceive different sounds, bilingual infants have to discriminate more possibilities (there are more speech sounds when there are two languages), but they seem to do so very efficiently. For example, Janet Werker and her team found that infants raised in a bilingual environment establish the phonetic representations for each of their languages in much the same manner, and on the same time course, as infants establishing representations for one language.[3] However, if there are many similar sounds (for example, Spanish and Catalan between them have three "e" sounds, as in "bet"), then bilingual infants may take a bit more time learning to discriminate them appropriately.[4]

As for when the first word is spoken, we've known for quite some time that monolingual and bilingual children do not differ; this takes place at around eleven months, on average.[5] The development of two vocabularies by bilingual children also seems to follow the pattern found in all children. One expert on the question, Barbara Zurer Pearson, wrote to me that bilinguals are right on target with onset milestones, on the condition that they don't have just cursory exposure to one of their two languages.[6] They need good exposure to both languages. In a study she conducted with Sylvia Fernandez, the bilingual children were reported to have 60 to 65 percent exposure in one language and 35 to 40 percent exposure in the other language—a difference that may explain why their vocabularies in the two languages were not equal. But all of the children showed the traditional "lexical spurt" (when a vocabulary increases suddenly) either alternately, depending on the strength of each language, or when both languages were taken together in the count.[7] Other researchers working on other aspects of language development have also reported similarities between monolingual and bilingual children: sounds or sound groups that are easier to produce appear sooner than those that are more difficult, some words are overextended (for example, when "doggie" is used to mean small four-legged animals), utterances slowly increase in length, simpler grammatical constructions are used before more complex ones, and so on.

In the preceding chapter, I mentioned little Hildegard, Werner Leopold's English-German bilingual daughter whose progress in her two languages was carefully documented by her father. In his very scholarly work, he raised an issue that is still heavily debated in the literature today—and that is of interest to parents. He stated that during her first two years, Hildegard combined her two languages into one system: her speech sounds belonged to a unified set, he wrote, undifferentiated by language. She also mixed English and German words, he stated, and failed to separate the two languages when speaking to monolingual English or German speakers. He added that it was only at the end of her second year that there appeared the "first flicker of the later unfolding of two separate language systems," and from then on she slowly began to distinguish between them.[8] The debate that Leopold's findings evoke is between two opposite positions: those who say bilingual children develop a single, unitary language system at the start that then slowly separates into two systems, and those who believe that bilingual children develop a dual, differentiated system from the very beginning.

Proponents of the one-system position point to the kind of evidence found by Leopold, such as the fact that bilingual children may "mix" their languages, sometimes more so in their early years than later on (we will come back to this point in the next chapter). There is also the fact that they sometimes use a single rule or device that can come from one or the other language. Another finding is that some bilingual children show little overlap in their two vocabularies (that is, a concept is represented by a word in one or the other language but rarely in both). For example, linguists Virginia Volterra and Traute Taeschner, who studied the vocabulary development of two little German-Italian bilinguals, Lisa and Giulia, found that Lisa had just three corresponding words (equivalents in the two languages) out of a vocabulary of eighty-seven words, and Giulia had six corresponding words out of an eighty-three-word vocabulary.[9] There is also the fact that blends and compounds are used by children in these early stages. For example, little Juliette, a two-year-old English-French bilingual, blended the French word *chaud* and its English equivalent "hot" into "shot." She also blended the English word "pickle" and its French equivalent, *cornichon*, to get "pinichon." As for compounds, Hildegard would say "Bitte-please" and Pierre, a French-English bilingual boy, produced "papa-daddy" and "chaud-hot."

Proponents of the alternate model, that children have two different languages from the start, are currently more numerous, and they have good arguments. For example, as early as 1976, Coral Bergman reported that her daughter Mary, in acquiring Spanish and English simultaneously, clearly differentiated her two languages at a very early age (fifteen months), responding in Spanish to her babysitter and in English to her mother. Bergman proposed this independent-development hypothesis:

> As it is being acquired, each language is able to develop independently of the other with the same pattern of acquisition as is found in monolingual children learning that language.[10]

Since then, researchers such as Jürgen Meisel, Annick De Houwer, and Fred Genesee, among many others, have defended a dual language system from the start. Jürgen Meisel, who actually talks of multiple first-language acquisition, states that children acquiring two languages simultaneously can differentiate the grammatical systems of their languages from very early on and without apparent effort. He then argues that the mixing bilingual children do around age two or just after can be explained, for the most part, as code-switching (see the next chapter). He states that these children master morphology correctly (they do not randomly attach inflectional morphemes from both languages to lexical material from each of the languages being acquired) and they follow the syntactic rules of these languages (for example, specific Romance language word-order patterns are never used in German by young French-German bilinguals).[11]

Where do we stand, then, on this issue? The two languages in the young bilingual are definitely in some form of contact but not in a state of "fusion," which could explain some of the observations made by earlier proponents of the unitary language position. Jürgen Meisel points out that the two languages do not develop at the same pace and this leads to such cross-linguistic influence as interference (transfer) and acceleration or delay in the acquisition of specific constructions. Researchers Virginia Yip and Stephen Matthews, who studied young Cantonese-English bilinguals, observed the pervasive influence of the dominant language on the weaker language, as well as some structures developing more quickly in one language due to their simplicity or transparency. They conclude that the bilingual children they studied—and this is probably true of most of these types of children—have a distinct and unique linguistic profile that cannot be characterized as a composite of two monolinguals housed in the same mind.[12]

Let me make one final point on the simultaneous acquisition of two languages. In order to clearly differentiate each language, children rely on different factors: the phonetic and prosodic cues (for example, the rhythm) of each language, other structural aspects, the context the language is used in, and, most importantly, the language spoken by a given person. Anyone who interacts for some time with a young bilingual child will notice the strong bond that exists for that child between a person and his or her language (the person-language bond). In the eyes of the child, a person is associated with one particular language, and if that person addresses the child in the other language, the child may refuse to answer or may be distressed. Here are two examples. Little Luca, bilingual in

French and Croatian, was speaking to his paternal grandmother. Their language of communication is French but since they were in Croatia, his grandmother asked him to name a few things in Croatian. He refused to do so and then said, in French, "It's mummy who asks that" (Luca speaks Croatian only to his mother and her parents). Juliette, a two-and-a-half-year-old French-English bilingual, was playing with Marc, a five-year-old English-speaking boy. Their usual language of communication was English, but to please and surprise her, Marc decided to use a French word with her. He asked his mother for the equivalent of "come" in French and then returned to Juliette and said, "Viens, viens." Much to his surprise, Juliette was far from pleased; instead of smiling, she said angrily, "Don't *do* that, Marc," and repeated this several times. Thus, it would seem that one strategy used by the bilingual child is to determine which language is spoken with whom, and to keep to that language. This makes the choice of words and of rules simpler and less effortful. When the person-language bond is broken, the young child is at a loss and may become upset.

Successive Bilingualism

As we have seen, most children become bilingual in a successive manner. That is, they learn one language in the home and then a second language at school or in the outside community. They therefore already have a language when they start acquiring the second one, and they can use their first language, to some extent at least (researchers diverge on the extent), in acquiring the new language.

Before describing how second-language acquisition takes place naturally in children, I will address a well-established misapprehension:

Myth: The earlier a language is acquired, the more fluent a child will be in it.

One assumption this myth is based on is the idea that young children acquire a language more quickly and with less effort than older children. Another is that the brain is more malleable or "plastic" very early on and hence is more receptive to such tasks as language learning. In addition, younger children are said to have fewer inhibitions, to be less embarrassed when they make mistakes, and hence to be better learners.

The reality is slightly different and this needs to be underscored. First, as applied linguist Barry McLaughlin reminds us, children do not have fewer inhibitions and are not less embarrassed when they make mistakes; in fact, they may well be shy and self-conscious in front of their peers.[13] Second, it has been shown that young children are rather unsophisticated and immature learners in that they have not yet fully acquired certain cognitive skills—such as the capacity to abstract, generalize, infer, and classify—that could help them in second-language acquisition. Third, the notion that there is a strict, critical period for language learning around the age of five years old has been replaced with the notion of a broader "sensitive period" that can extend beyond ten years old and is probably different for different language skills.

Thus, in a well-known study, researchers Catherine Snow and Marianne Hoefnagel-Hohle examined the learning of Dutch by speakers of English in different age groups. They showed that twelve- to fifteen-year-olds did better than younger learners.[14] The only real advantage for acquiring a language at an early age is in pronunciation skills, but as we saw in Chapter 7, even teenagers and some adults can learn to speak without an accent. In sum, the crucial factors for becoming bilingual as a child, at whatever age, are the need for the new language, as well as the amount and type of input, the role of the family and the school, and the prevailing attitudes toward the language and the culture and toward bilingualism as such.[15]

In her work, linguist Lily Wong Fillmore proposed a description or model of natural second-language learning in children. Its particular interest lies in the fact that she deals with young second-language learners who are members of immigrant families. Her description, however, is applicable to many other bilingual children, so long as they acquire their second language naturally. These learners already speak one language at home and they have a need to learn the majority language. By so doing, they become bilingual, one hopes for the rest of their lives—although, as we saw in the previous chapter, this may not be the case if they start losing their first language. Wong Fillmore stresses, first of all, that these children do not come to the task empty-handed; they already possess social, linguistic, and world knowledge; they know what language is used for and what settings it is used in. All of this is of great help to them in learning the new language.[16]

Wong Fillmore's model has three components and three sets of processes. The components are the learners who know they have to acquire the second language, the speakers of the language who will help them do so in various ways, and the social setting that brings the learners and speakers into contact—the school, above all, but also the community. As for the processes, the first set in the model concerns social aspects. The learners have to observe what is happening in social settings and figure out what people are talking about and how they do it. They also have to make the speakers aware of their needs and get them to make accommodations and adjustments so that they can understand the speakers, and so that they can acquire the language. In a word, both sides have to cooperate. In her earlier work, Lily Wong Fillmore described three social strategies used by language learners: (1) join a group and act as if you understand what is going on, even if you don't; (2) give the impression, with a few well-chosen words, that you can speak the language; and (3) count on your friends for help.[17]

Here is an example of how ten-year-old Cyril used these strategies. After having gone through several years of monolingualism, Cyril moved with his parents to the French-speaking part of Switzerland and entered the village school a month after his arrival. Because he was American (at least culturally) and was fun to be with, he was an immediate success. However, his French at the start was nonexistent and his friends' English was no better. So for a few weeks he applied Wong Fillmore's strategies, without knowing that's what he was doing, of course. He quickly learned a few set expressions and used them along with gestures—and a big smile. His new friends, in turn, did all they could to help him out. One of the ways they did this was by simplifying their French considerably. At the local village fair, for example, kids could "fish" for a present that an adult, behind a screen, would put on the hook. One of the prizes Cyril wanted was a rubber alligator. Knowing this, one of the French-speaking children said to Cyril in "broken" French: "Moi avoir alligator, te donner" (literally, "Me get alligator, I give you"). The sentence he would normally have used with a French-speaking friend would have been much more complex, of the type, "Si j'obtiens l'alligator, je te le donnerai." Cyril understood the simplified sentence and all was well (but I don't believe he ever did get the alligator).

The second set of processes Lily Wong Fillmore mentions concerns linguistic aspects. Again without being aware that they are doing it, learners have to obtain from native speakers information to allow them to discover how the language works and how people use it. They get this information from the redundant, repetitive, and regular speech that is spoken to them in context by native speakers. The learners have to pay close attention to what is being said and assume a relationship between that and the events around them. They make educated guesses about what people are saying and what they are likely to talk about in a given situation. As Wong Fillmore puts it: "Assume that what people are saying is directly relevant to the situation at hand or to what they or you are experiencing. (Metastrategy: guess)."[18] Learners bring to the task their knowledge of linguistic categories, types of structures (declarative, interrogative, and so on), and speech acts (direct and indirect), and hence they can look for their equivalents in the new language.

Finally, cognitive elements form the third set of processes. For Wong Fillmore these are central, as they result in the acquisition of the language. Given the contextual input they are obtaining, learners must discover the units and rules of the language; they must then synthesize this knowledge into a grammar. They apply cognitive skills to accomplish this, such as associative and analytical skills, memory, inferential skills, and so on. They also use learning strategies, some of which Wong Fillmore lists: "Look for recurring parts in the formulas you know"; "Make the most of what you've got"; "Work on big things; save the details for later."[19]

A point made by many language acquisition specialists, including Lily Wong Fillmore and Barry McLaughlin, concerns the fact that learners can be very different from one another. They may come from different cultural, linguistic, and social groups; they may be of different ages; they may have different cognitive abilities (for example, perceptual skills, pattern recognition skills), as well as different attitudes toward trying new things and taking risks. Some will indeed actively venture forth, even if they make mistakes, while others will be more reserved, and sometimes the outcome of the latter approach may be more successful. Let me cite the example of two brothers, Cyril, whom we have already met, and Pierre, both English-speaking boys acquiring French in a natural setting. Cyril was ten and his brother was five. Whereas Cyril was a very outgoing, let's-try-it kind of boy, Pierre was much more reserved and quiet. Cyril acquired broken French very quickly; he would make pronunciation errors, gender errors, grammatical errors, but he wouldn't mind, and he just kept communicating with his friends. Pierre used a different approach. For about three months he hardly said a word in French (he even managed to get his teacher to speak basic English to him), but when he did start to speak French freely, it was much more error free than Cyril's French. It was as if Pierre had let the language settle in, following the path described by Wong Fillmore, and then, once everything was in place (grammar, pronunciation, vocabulary), he set about speaking the language. He even had the nerve to correct his older brother at times. For example, the latter said *formage* one day instead of *fromage* (cheese), and much to Cyril's annoyance, Pierre butted in and said, "C'est fromage, Cyril!"

As an end to this chapter, I would like to stress a very important aspect of second-language learning that is underlined by many specialists in the domain, most notably Jim Cummins. Attaining communicative abilities in a second language in a natural environment is only part of the process schoolchildren have to go through, since most times they need to read and write the language as well as speak it. Conversational fluency (what Cummins calls "basic interpersonal communicative skills") is attained quite quickly if the setting is right and all goes well (for example, both Cyril and Pierre were fluent in conversational spoken French after a year in Switzerland). This is true for many young bilinguals and may give the impression that they have acquired the new language. But academic language proficiency (what Cummins calls "cognitive academic language proficiency") takes much more time and work.[20] As Cummins writes, monolingual children with normal language development come to school at age four or five fluent in their home language; they then spend the next twelve years expanding their linguistic competence in the sphere of literacy (which includes not only reading and writing but also being able to use language, as well as viewing, representing, and thinking about ideas critically). Academic language is complex, Cummins reminds us, because of the difficulty of the concepts that have to be understood, the uncommon and technical vocabulary that has to be known, and the sophisticated grammatical constructions that have to be used. Cummins estimates that second-language learners require some five years to catch up to their native-language peers in literacy-related language skills.[21] As we will see in Chapter 17, they also need strong family and teacher support to manage this.

16

Linguistic Aspects of Childhood Bilingualism

When one talks about bilingual children with others, a number of topics invariably turn up: dominance in a language, adapting to the language mode, and language "mixing." In this chapter we will take up these topics and also discuss bilingual children as natural interpreters. Finally, we will look at how bilingual children play with languages.

Dominance in a Language

Bilingual children often show signs of dominance in a language. There are several reasons for this, related to whether children acquire their two languages simultaneously or learn one language after the other. When languages are acquired simultaneously, it may happen that certain linguistic constructs are more complex in one language than in the other and hence are acquired more quickly in the "easier" language, thereby giving the impression that the child is dominant in that language. For example, children bilingual in Hungarian and Serbian may express location earlier in Hungarian than in Serbian, since in Hungarian it is expressed with only an inflection on the noun, whereas Serbian requires an inflection on the noun and a locative preposition.[1] Linguist Marilyn Vihman found something similar in the speech of little Raivo, an Estonian-English bilingual child. He had a tendency to omit bound morphemes in Estonian (endings such as -da or -ega) because morphology in Estonian is more complex than in English and he took more time acquiring it.[2]

Apart from these structural reasons, language dominance in children acquiring two languages simultaneously is mainly due to the amount of exposure they get in each language. It is common for a child to receive more input in one language than to receive equal inputs in the two. We saw in Chapter 14, for example, that Hildegard was dominant in English before her trip to Germany; not only did her mother speak English to her but it was also the language of the environment. This was also true for Stephen who, for a while, was dominant in Garo. The main effect of dominance—which can change, sometimes quite quickly—is that the stronger language develops to a greater extent than the weaker one (more sounds are isolated, more words are acquired, more grammatical rules are inferred) and it has a tendency to influence the weaker language. Robbins Burling reported that his son Stephen, for example, used Garo phonemes instead of English phonemes when he spoke English.[3] Usually the influence is not total, as with Stephen, but only partial. Thus little Anne, an English-French bilingual child whose dominant language was English, would translate the English prepositions that are used with English verbs and add them to French verbs. She would say, for example, "Je cherche *pour* le livre" based on "I'm looking *for* the book" instead of the grammatically correct "Je cherche le livre."[4]

Language dominance in children acquiring two languages successively is even more pervasive than in their younger counterparts who are raised with two languages from the start, since at first they only have one language and it is constantly present when they are acquiring and speaking the second language. Of course, learning to speak a second language isn't just a question of being influenced constantly by the first language. Linguists have known for a long time that some processes of second-language acquisition resemble those of first-language acquisition: using simple structures before more complex ones, overextending the meaning of words, simplifying the morphology, overgeneralizing rules, simplifying various linguistic constructs, and so on. Thus, for example, when a young second-language learner says, "I taked the bus with Mummy," she is overgeneralizing the regular past-tense rule in English to irregular verbs. And when a young French learner says, "Moi malade" (I sick) he is simplifying the French utterance, "Je suis malade," by using *moi* for all instances of the first person and omitting the verb. That said, the first language is ever present, as can be seen in the many interferences (or transfers) that children make. Ten-year-old Cyril, when acquiring French, produced sentences that were clearly influenced by English. For example, he would say, "Pas toucher mon nez," based on "Don't touch my nose" instead of "N(e) me touche pas le nez." He also said, "Maintenant dit papa la chanson" based on "Now tell Daddy the song" instead of "Maintenant dit la chanson à papa."

It is important to view within- and between-language mechanisms (overgeneralizations, simplifications, interferences, and so on) as strategies employed by children in their effort to use their weaker language. Further language input and feedback from listeners, as well as occasional breakdowns in communication, will gradually help the child home in on the new language.

Adapting to the Language Mode

We saw in Chapter 4 that in their everyday lives, bilinguals find themselves at various points along a situational continuum that induces different language modes. At one end of the continuum, bilinguals are in a monolingual mode because they are speaking to monolinguals in one—or the other—of the languages that they know. They therefore have to use the correct language and exclude (deactivate) the other language. At the other end of the continuum, bilinguals find themselves in a bilingual language mode because they are communicating with bilinguals who share their two languages. They have to choose which language to use and they can also code-switch and borrow if their interlocutors accept this behavior and the situation is appropriate. Children quickly learn about language mode and become adept at language choice and code-switching.

Concerning language choice, I will mention two little children, Mario and Carla, who acquired English and Spanish simultaneously. Their father, anthropologist and linguist Alvino Fantini, describes the factors that guided his children's choice of language. They were very much like those that guide adults. For example, when the children knew their interlocutor, they spoke to him or her in the appropriate language. When that was not the case, then the environment was the important factor. In a Spanish environment (in Mexico or Bolivia, for example) they would use Spanish. In an English environment (say, the United States) they would use English—but only if they knew that the person did not speak Spanish. The telephone, the radio, and the television were all extensions of the setting for them; thus they showed surprise when they heard a Spanish voice on the radio in Vermont. If they didn't know their interlocutor but he or she looked "Latin," then they would start out in Spanish but would switch over to English if the other person did not respond. The person's level of fluency was also an important factor—and something they could judge by age four. If Mario and Carla noticed that the person was using his or her weaker language to communicate with them, then they would inevitably choose the other language.[5] (Unlike adults, children are not prepared to allow a person to practice his or her weaker language with them.) Fantini's study, along with others, shows that young bilingual children rapidly develop a decision process wherein the interlocutor is the primary factor for language choice, followed by the situation and the function of the interaction. Other factors, such as the topic of interaction, appear later.

Children quickly learn to what extent code-switching behavior is permissible in an interaction. Psycholinguist Elizabeth Lanza recorded a two-year-old Norwegian-English bilingual child (Siri) interacting with her American mother and then her Norwegian father, both of whom were bilingual. What is interesting is that the mother frequently feigned the role of a monolingual and did not code-switch languages with Siri. The father, on the other hand, accepted Siri's language code-switching and responded to it. Lanza analyzed the interactions between Siri and her parents in terms of a monolingual- to bilingual-discourse context continuum, along which she placed various parental strategies. For example, she placed "minimal grasp" and "expressed guess" at the monolingual end of the continuum; they were precisely the strategies used by the mother. With the first strategy, minimal grasp, the adult indicates no comprehension of the child's other language, and with the second, the parent asks a yes-no question using the other language. At the bilingual end, one finds two other strategies: "move on," where the conversation is allowed to continue (indicating the adult has understood the element from the other language), and "code-switching," where the adult also code-switches with the child (these were the strategies used by Siri's father). Overall during the period of the study (from age two years to two and a half), the strategies produced very different results: Siri brought in many more words of the other language with her father, who was open to code-switching, than with her mother, who did not respond to it. What this means in terms of language mode is that Siri was probably in different modes with her two parents—she leaned toward the monolingual mode with her mother but never reached it, as she did switch with her sometimes, and she was at the bilingual end of the continuum with her father.[6]

The sociolinguist Erica McClure has studied code-switching for many years. Examples from her early work with Mexican American children are particularly interesting. In addition to observing switches used to fill lexical gaps, she found switches aimed at resolving ambiguities or clarifying statements in the speech of children as young as three years old. She also found that the younger children used switches to attract or retain attention, as in: "Yo me voy a bajar, Teresa [I'm getting down, Teresa]. *Look!*" Switches for emphasis occurred only later, at ages eight or nine, as in, "Stay here, Roli. *Te quedas aquí* [you stay here]." Other late-occurring switches were those used for elaboration and those involving focus, such as topicalization; for example: "*Este Ernesto* [this Ernest], he's cheating."[7] Cristina Banfi mentions instances of code-switching she observed in her three-and-a-half-year-old English-Spanish bilingual daughter, Anabel. In one of them, Anabel realizes that there are some monolinguals present in the bilingual group she is addressing. Since she wants to include them in the surprise she is presenting, she says, "Ciérrense los ojos. *Close your eyes*."[8] In sum, children acquire code-switching skills early on, and they use them when in a bilingual mode to fill a linguistic need, and also as a communicative strategy.

Language "Mixing" in Bilingual Children

Myth: Children raised bilingual will always mix their languages.

Language mixing is widely viewed as a consequence of bilingualism in children. The problem is that it is unclear what is meant by "mixing." I have tried to keep away from this word myself because it has so many meanings. Are we talking about interferences in language-dominant children? Do we mean code-switches and borrowings, or even a change in the base language, in children who are in a bilingual language mode? In addition, the word carries the connotation that the language being spoken by bilingual children is somehow tainted. In fact, there are a number of factors that may account for the greater presence of the other language and the "mixing" that results.

As we have seen, bilingual children may be dominant in one language (whether they are simultaneous or successive bilinguals), and that language has a tendency to "impose itself" on the weaker language. This can take the form of interferences and also the direct use of elements of the dominant language to fill various gaps in the weaker language (words, in particular). Psycholinguist Fred Genesee and his collaborators showed this clearly in a study in which they observed five French-English children between the ages of twenty-two and twenty-six months who were being raised bilingual. Three were language-dominant children. Oli was French dominant and Ban and Tan were English dominant. Oli showed a relatively high rate of French elements in the English he spoke with his English-speaking mother (English was his weaker language), whereas Ban and Tan showed the reverse: more English elements when speaking French to their father (French was their weaker language).[9]

As for successive bilinguals, children who first acquire one language and then the other, we have already seen that they will go through a period of language dominance. They will produce interferences, and they will insert elements of their stronger language into their weaker language as a stop-gap measure. But as soon as they have picked up enough of the second language, they will increasingly speak just that language and will then call on the other language mainly for communicative reasons, primarily when the situation is appropriate and they are in a bilingual mode.

Language mode is precisely another factor that accounts for language mixing. First, it is not yet clear at what age children start to control their movement along the monolingual-bilingual continuum as well as their bilingual speech. We saw above that this seems to take place quite early on, but there may be a short period of adjustment when language choice and code-switching mechanisms are not yet under control. Slippage can take place at this point, and hence the mixing. Second, with older children, it is unclear what language mode they are in when mixing takes place. If they are speaking to adults who know their two languages, even if only one language is being used, then it is not surprising that they bring in the other language. Children are terribly pragmatic: if they are supposed to use a particular language with a particular adult but they know that she also speaks their other language, then they may well bring in that language in case of need. More generally, when children grow up in families where everyday communication is bilingual speech with a lot of base-language changes and code-switching, it is no surprise that the young children speak in a similar fashion. As we will see in the next chapter, it is important for bilingual children to obtain monolingual input in each of their languages when they are young, even if they receive bilingual input from time to time. Monolingual speech allows them to learn that in some situations, mainly with monolinguals, one has to speak just one language, whereas in other situations one can use both languages.

Bilingual Children as Interpreters

One aspect of bilingual children that simply amazes people, even researchers like me, is their ability to interpret quite early on. We have seen in earlier chapters that interpretation is a very complex skill. We all realize that children do not have the same interpretation capacities as adults, nor the necessary vocabulary in both languages, but nevertheless their natural ability in this domain never ceases to impress us. Brian Harris and Bianca Sherwood describe a young Italian girl (referred to as BS) who, before she was four, was already interpreting between the Abruzzi dialect (her mother's only language) and Italian (her father's language; he also spoke the Abruzzi dialect). When BS and her family moved to Venezuela and opened a grocery store, BS greeted customers in Spanish, which she had learned in no time, and could interpret messages from them to either parent. The family then emigrated to Canada and BS, who was then eight, added English to her three other languages. She continued translating and interpreting for her parents: phone calls, conversations, messages, mail, newspaper articles, and TV programs. For the latter, she used either successive interpretation, in which she would give the gist of the information, or simultaneous interpretation, a more difficult form of translation.[10]

Like many children with minority-language parents, BS would act as a liaison between her parents and the outside, majority-language-speaking environment. Not only would she translate but also, as she grew older, she drew on her bicultural skills to explain why things were done the way they were. Some situations she found herself in were difficult. Her father would get worked up in bargaining sessions with non-Italians and become angry and upset. She would have to soften his outbursts at the risk of having her father get angry at her, since he had some comprehension of English. Here is a typical exchange presented by Harris and Sherwood:

> *Father to BS (in Italian):* Tell him he's a nitwit.
> *BS to third party (in English):* My father won't accept your offer.
> *Father angrily to BS (in Italian):* Why didn't you tell him what I told you?[11]

Many bilingual children find themselves in BS's situation. The ones that have particularly fascinated me are the hearing children of Deaf parents who grow up with sign language and the majority oral language. In the following extract, an American Sign Language–English bilingual relates how she first became an interpreter at age four and how she used her interpreting skills at the doctor's office and when making long-distance phone calls for her parents:

> There is nothing that stands out in my mind about being
> bilingual as a child with the possible exception of being
> an interpreter at four years of age. That was the main dif-

ference between myself and most other kids; I had to go home to interpret at the doctor's office for grandma or whoever it was that day. One problem I did encounter many, many times was making long-distance calls. In those days, there was no dial-direct service, and trying to make an operator believe a four- to six-year-old who was trying to call Virginia from Boston was always a problem. Everyone wanted to speak to my "mommy." People who called the house and specifically asked for any member of my family never knew how to handle the situation when faced with having to discuss an adult problem with a nine-year-old.[12]

Although for some children interpreting is a game, it can also be hard work if not a burden, and adults should be careful not to ask too much of them. Harris and Sherwood tell us about HB, a seven-year-old French-Bulgarian bilingual who was taken to visit a Bulgarian family that had just arrived in Canada. He was left with the family's child to watch TV in French. When his mother came back to fetch him, he told her he was tired because he had interpreted the program into Bulgarian for his playmate. Paul Preston, in his interviews with adult children of Deaf parents, found that a recurring theme was the fact that they had to interpret for their parents. Some had negative memories of this, like Thelma:

I hated it when [my mother's] friends came over . . . and wanted me to be their interpreter for them to go to the bank, take care of their business . . . I was the community interpreter. I was put in situations I didn't know I could say no to.[13]

Some others found various ways of making their interpreting life a bit more manageable. Preston tells us that telephone interpreting offered the greatest latitude in manipulating conversations, as it placed the communication in the hands of the hearing child. George, for example, was asked by his father to call up all the garage mechanics in the Yellow Pages in order to compare prices. This is what he did:

> I tried to tell him that there were just too many, but he insisted. So, I sat there and pretended to be talking to someone when it was just the dial tone.[14]

Many parents do realize the burden they are placing on their bilingual children. Preston tells us about Tom, who one day was angry with his mother for asking him to interpret; she responded by signing:

> I know, hard on you. Hard on me too. Hard on both of us. Not like hearing people. They have an easier life.[15]

Researchers have begun to study the interpreting abilities of young bilingual children, and their results confirm the children's skills. For example, Marguerite Malakoff and Kenji Hakuta examined the abilities of young English-Spanish bilinguals (ages ten and eleven) in New Haven, Connecticut. They found that the children made very few errors; the main ones were missing words because they did not have the equivalent in the language they were translating into. Of course, they were more efficient when translating into their dominant language (English) than into their nondominant one (Spanish). The authors concluded that interpretation skills are widely found in bilingual children by late elementary school.[16]

In a later study, Stanford University professor Guadalupe Valdés examined the strategies adopted by Spanish-English bilingual youngsters when asked to interpret in a rather unusual situation: a simulated meeting between a Spanish-speaking mother and the English-speaking principal of the daughter's school because the daughter has been accused of stealing. The majority of the youngsters involved in the study had been identified as interpreters in their family and community. Valdés found that these young interpreters succeeded in keeping up with the information flow; they used a number of strategies to convey essential information, including tone and stance, and they were able to compensate for linguistic limitations. She concluded that the traits and abilities they exhibited were characteristic of exceptionally cognitively competent individuals—in this case, gifted children.[17]

Playing with Languages

Play is something that one overlooks when talking about bilingual children and their languages. Just like monolingual children who play with language (making words rhyme, inventing new words, and so on), bilingual children play with their two (or more) languages. For example, they may jokingly speak to a person in the wrong language. Alvino Fantini relates that Mario and Carla would tease their grandparents by speaking to them in Spanish instead of English. They would also speak to their parents in the wrong language, English, to amuse them (the home language was Spanish).[18]

Children also play with code-switching and borrowing, especially when it is frowned upon in the family. Thus, Yves Gentilhomme, who grew up as a French-Russian bilingual, tells us that his bilingual friends and he had fun borrowing French words into Russian and giving them Russian morphological endings. For example, the French *assiette* (plate) adapted into Russian with the accusative marker would give them: "Daj mne asjetu" (Give me a plate). Another game consisted in translating idiomatic expressions literally into the other language and producing them with a straight face. An example given by Gentilhomme was calling someone "my little cabbage" in Russian (a direct translation of "mon petit chou," which in French means "my little lamb").[19]

Children are quite aware of pronunciation and play with it a lot. They sometimes make fun of people who speak a language with an accent by repeating what they said and adding their accent. Cristina Banfi tells us that little Anabel plays with this aspect of language; here is an exchange between Anabel and her father, who is English speaking:

> *Anabel:* Dad, how do you say Harry Potter in Spanish?
> *Father:* There is no translation. It's the same.
> *Anabel:* No, Dad, it's "Harry Potter" (pronounced as it is in Spanish).[20]

17

Family Strategies and Support

Making children bilingual, and keeping them that way, is a responsibility that many families give a lot of thought to. Admittedly, some children "just become bilingual" (I was one of those when I was put into an English boarding school at age eight), but an increasing number of parents are concerned about the approach they should adopt, and the support they should give their children, in order to ease their way into a life with two or more languages. In this chapter, we will discuss the family strategies that are available and the support that bilingual children, and parents, should receive. I include in the concept of "family" parents and grandparents, as well as more distant family members and other caretakers.

Family Strategies

I have met many couples who want to start a family and are wondering how best to make sure their children are bilingual. The reasons they give for raising bilingual children are many: some want them to be able to speak both the parents' languages (for example, the mother speaks Spanish and the father English); others want them to be able to communicate with their grandparents; some want to prepare them for the day they will enter school, where a different language is used; and still others want to give them a head start in languages. Whatever the reason, they are looking for ways to start their children on the road to bilingualism.

There are five strategies that parents can follow to promote bilingualism in their children. Probably the best-known is the "one person–one language" strategy, which was made famous in the world of bilingualism (even though it had probably existed for centuries) when, at the beginning of the twentieth century, Jules Ronjat asked French linguist Maurice Grammont how best to bring up his child to be bilingual. Ronjat's wife was German and he was French. Grammont proposed that each parent should speak his or her language exclusively to baby Louis, and that is what they did. Ronjat later wrote a book on the strategy and stated that Louis had acquired each language just as any native-speaking child would have done. Recall that little Hildegard, whom we met in Chapter 14, was raised with the same strategy; her father spoke German to her and her mother spoke English.

A second strategy is to use one language in the home, usually the minority language, and the other language outside the home (I will call this the "home–outside the home" strategy). The idea is that everyone in the home speaks only one language so that it is acquired well; as for the other language, it will be acquired when the child ventures outside the home and, later, when he or she goes to day care and then enters school. This approach is used—although not, perhaps, as a conscious strategy—by millions of immigrant families in which the minority language is spoken in the home, and sometimes also in the neighborhood, and the majority language is spoken in the outside society. When parents consciously adopt this strategy for their children, they usually enforce the home–outside the home dichotomy much more strictly. The well-known bilingualism specialist Einar Haugen was brought up bilingual in Norwegian and English with this approach. He writes:

> [My parents] took the position that I would learn all the
> English I needed from my playmates and my teachers,
> and that only by learning and using Norwegian in the
> home could I maintain a fruitful contact with them and
> their friends and their culture.[1]

A third strategy consists of first using one language with the child and then later, around age four or five, introducing the other language. I will call this the "one-language-first" strategy. Usually, the first language is the minority language, which the parents use exclusively. They make sure that every contact the child has (other caretakers, family members, playmates, television, and so on) takes place in that language. Once that language is well established, then parents allow the other language to be acquired, and this usually happens very fast if it is the majority language of the outside community.

A fourth strategy—the "language-time" strategy—is to use one language at specific times (for example, in the morning) and the other at other times (say, in the afternoon). The alternating can be done on the same day or over several days (perhaps by speaking one language during the first part of the week, another language during the second part).

The fifth strategy, which is a kind of default strategy even though it is adopted consciously by parents, is to use the two languages interchangeably, letting such factors as topic, person, situation, and so forth dictate the language to be used. I will call this the "free-alternation" strategy.

What is the rate of success of these different strategies? As concerns the first, the one person–one language strategy, we should note that it is adopted by many parents who feel more comfortable speaking their dominant language—maybe the only language for one of them—with their child. It is certainly the best-known strategy, but the perception people have of it has evolved, over time, into a mistaken belief:

Myth: If parents want their children to grow up bilingual, they should use the one person–one language approach.

One person–one language is certainly a fine strategy in the very first months of language development, when children are primarily with their parents. They obtain dual language input and, very quickly, they produce sounds, and then syllables and words, in both languages. The problem, though, is that one language, the minority language, will eventually have less and less input unless the parents take very clear action. As soon as the children go out into the outside world (unless they live in a minority community with the minority language), they will hear and use the other, majority language much more. In addition to the problem of decreased input in the minority language, children will want to be like other children and not be singled out. So, little by little, the majority language will start taking over, much to the distress of the parent who uses the minority language. Childhood bilingualism expert Annick De Houwer conducted a large survey covering close to two thousand families and found that there was a one-in-four chance that children would fail to speak the minority language when this strategy was used.[2] In sum, I am not an unconditional supporter of the one person–one language strategy, as the child may well receive decreasing input from the minority language; this makes the life of the minority-language parent difficult and can create stress in the family.

The home–outside the home strategy has a few inconveniences but many advantages. Among the inconveniences is the fact that one of the parents will probably have to agree to speak his or her second (or third) language to the child so that everyone is speaking just one language in the home. Another inconvenience is that, after a while, the home language—usually the minority language—will need to be reinforced with input from friends and other family members, as well as activities in that language, such as playing in the language and watching TV programs in it. If this reinforcement can be achieved, then the other, outside-the-home language, which is usually the majority language, will take care of itself—in day care and then school, through outside friends, and so on—and the children will become bilingual. Parents will then have to work on stabilizing the languages and making sure that a need for them continues to exist throughout the childhood and adolescent years (see Chapter 14). In her survey, Annick De Houwer found that if both parents used the same language in the home, then the success of transmitting that language, along with the outside language, increased by 20 percent.

What about the one-language-first strategy? This approach is successful when the family is surrounded by a well-organized and quite large minority-language community so that the child is given all the language input he or she needs. If that is not the case, it may be difficult to avoid having the majority language come in earlier. Here is the testimony of a Russian-English bilingual who was raised with this strategy in the United States. She first learned Russian at home and acquired English when she entered school:

I didn't speak a word of English when I first went to school. There was another little boy entering kindergarten with me, but our mothers separated us so that we wouldn't speak Russian between ourselves. I can't specifically remember learning English; I seem to have picked it up very quickly.[3]

As for the language-time strategy, it is based on a very arbitrary factor, the time of day or the day of the week, and is not very successful, at least in the family setting. However, it is a strategy used in immersion and dual-language educational programs (see Chapter 19), and it is successful in that kind of environment.

The last strategy, the free-alternation strategy, is by far the most natural, but its success rate suffers from the fact that the majority language will become dominant as the child spends more time at school and outside the home, not to mention with the majority-language friends he or she will bring home.

Whichever strategy parents adopt, once bilingualism has started to take hold, the family has to keep monitoring the environment to ensure that the child has a real need for both languages, and that he or she is receiving enough exposure to both languages. Exposure should come from active human interaction (speaking to, playing with, or reading to the child) and not from passive activities such as watching TV or DVDs. To increase exposure to the languages, and to reduce the load put on parents, it is preferable if members of the extended family and other caretakers can help, and if the child can interact with other children who speak the languages.

There is one important aspect that parents have to be careful about. If at all possible, children must be able to find themselves, at various times, in a monolingual mode in each of their languages (see Chapter 4). This means that, unlike in the home, where at least one parent is bilingual (if not two), children should come into regular contact with monolingual speakers of each language. There are two reasons for this. First, children will receive input that does not contain code-switches and borrowings, those elements of the other language that often appear when bilinguals speak to one another. Second, it allows children to learn how to navigate along the monolingual-bilingual language-mode continuum and hence to adapt their speech to the situation and interlocutor. As we saw in the previous chapter, children quickly learn when to speak a particular language in a specific situation and, if the mode is monolingual, to deactivate their other language. In a bilingual home, it is simply too easy to slip into a bilingual mode: parents bring in words from the other language and sometimes even change over to the stronger language to speak to each another or to make sure they are understood by their children. Children have a tendency to copy their parents and, little by little, the dominant language increases its presence until it has replaced the minority language. Linguist and speech pathologist Susanne Döpke puts it very well in imagining how a child might decide to favor one language:

> Mummy speaks English or Greek to me and everybody
> else speaks English to me. Consequently, I can choose to
> speak English or Greek to Mummy, but because I hear
> English much more than Greek, English is easier to use.
> So why should I use Greek?[4]

If families do not have a minority-language community at hand in which there are monolingual speakers, finding ways of putting children in a monolingual mode in the minority language is admittedly difficult and calls for some creativity. When they returned to the United States from Switzerland, the parents of Cyril and Pierre did several things to keep up their children's French and hence maintain their English-French bilingualism. For example, they sought out newly arrived French families who had children of the same age, and they put the children together to see if they would become friends. This worked with one or two of the French youngsters, and so for several months, while those children were acquiring English, Cyril and Pierre had French monolingual children speaking and playing with them in French. In addition, the parents invited the friends their boys had made in Switzerland to visit them in the United States over the summer. Since those friends were strictly monolingual, Cyril and Pierre had no choice but to speak French with them. Finally, the family tried to get over to Switzerland and France once a year so as to immerse Cyril and Pierre in their other, now weaker language.

What is interesting about the stratagems used by these parents is that they were quite natural. The children were put into situations where they needed their nondominant language and so they used it. Their bilingual parents learned rather quickly, as have many others, that forcing a child to keep to just one language when his or her interlocutor knows both only leads to frustration on both sides. I have often said, with a smile, that bilingual parents are far from being the best friends of their children's weaker language and hence of their bilingualism. But they can make up for this by putting their children in natural situations where they have a real need for their weaker language.

Family Support

Not only should bilingual children receive support from their family if at all possible (recall that I include parents and grandparents as well as more distant family members and other caretakers under this term), but also the family itself should get help from others. I am thinking of support from relatives and friends, and also from those who play an important role in the young child's world, such as teachers, doctors, psychologists, and language therapists. I remain astounded by the myths and stereotypes that are passed on to families and by the type of "advice" that they are given. For example, the literature is full of testimonies about teachers coming to minority-language homes to ask that the children not be raised bilingually and to say that the family should speak only the majority language, as Richard Rodriguez recounted in his memoir *Hunger of Memory*.[5]

How many parents, based on the advice of others—including professionals—have forced themselves to change their language behavior and thus deprived their children of becoming bilingual? Ray Castro speaks of his own experience very touchingly. He relates that at home, with his parents, aunt and uncle, and grandparents, the language was Spanish and the culture distinctly Mexican. His parents did everything they could so that he learned English, which he needed to survive in America. The problem was that it was done at the expense of Spanish. Castro explains that little by little his Spanish dwindled to nothing; he did not identify with the dominant culture nor with his Chicano culture, as he didn't have Spanish. He writes:

> I felt alone and lonely . . . My parents were not at fault;
> from them English was a gift of love—a gift they had
> never received. They were sure that I would not endure
> the suffering that accompanies such labels as foreigner
> or, in my case, *wetback* and *spic* . . . My years without
> Spanish now appear tragic. How can I ever make up that

loss! I barely communicated with my own grandparents!
They died, in fact, before I relearned Spanish.[6]

One cannot expect parents to develop the expertise in various aspects of bilingualism that linguists, educators, psychologists, speech therapists, and members of the medical world may have. But it is important that they be able to differentiate, with the help of these professionals, between the myths that surround the field and the reality. In addition, it is crucial that parents, and all those who take care of bilingual children, be informed about such topics as how children become bilingual and retain their bilingualism, what it means to be bilingual, the complementarity principle, language mode, code-switching and borrowing, the effects of bilingualism on children, and so on. This knowledge will help them comprehend the development of their bilingual children and prepare them for the appearance of various bilingual phenomena. For example, parents must understand why it is that some children go through a period when they refuse to speak the home language, in public and sometimes in the home, in large part because they do not wish to be different from other children. An Arabic-English bilingual wrote to me about this:

> As an adolescent I pretended I did not know Arabic, and I
> tried very hard to lose my foreign accent. I did this be-
> cause I wanted very badly not to be any different from
> the rest of my friends. As I got older, though, I started to
> learn and appreciate my native language and culture
> much more.[7]

Bilingual children are particularly conscious of their parents' sometimes broken knowledge of the majority language. Richard

Rodriguez speaks of being troubled by his parents' "high-whining" vowels and "guttural consonants" and their confused syntax. He would grow nervous hearing them speak English. And the journalist and writer Olivier Todd recounts how, in the streets and stores of Paris, he would pretend not to know his mother when she spoke with her strong British accent. I personally recall the day my son told me, "Dad, speak like all the other dads," by which he meant something like, "Since you also speak English, and English is the language used here, and I don't want to be different from the others, then let's speak English together instead of French."

In an interesting longitudinal study spanning six years, Stephen Caldas and Suzanne Caron-Caldas tracked language use in their three adolescent English-French bilingual children in both their Louisiana home and their Quebec summer residence. They showed that the home-language preference in Louisiana shifted from predominantly French to overwhelmingly English as they grew older, whereas in Quebec, the reverse was true and the language preference shifted totally to French. This was explained, they said, by peer influence outside the home, as their children had English-speaking peers in Louisiana and French-speaking peers in Quebec. In a revealing anecdote included in the study, the father, who spoke French to his children in Louisiana, was with his twelve-year-old daughter, Stéphanie, at a football game. He was getting ready to say hi to one of her friends when Stéphanie hissed to him, "Don't speak French to her." (The father did so anyway.) In the end, the children would no longer speak French to their parents in Louisiana but would do so with no problem in Quebec. While the authors refer to the "parallel monolingualism" of their children, the latter were in fact bilingual in a very specific way.[8]

While parents must be aware of what a child is going through as he or she is learning to live with two or more languages (languages that might not have the same social status), they must also understand the cultural changes that the child or adolescent is going through if they have moved from one country or region to another. Many children experience culture shock, as do their parents, and they need help during this transition phase. Author Nancy Huston remembers vividly the night she arrived, at the age of six, straight from Canada, at the German home of her new stepmother. She was offered traditional German food, including cold cuts, black bread, and various cheeses, but all this was foreign to her, as were the people around her and the language they spoke. She kept her head down and touched nothing on her plate. But one person was attuned to what she was living through. Her new aunt Wilma went out in the dark, drove some thirty miles, and found her a box of Kellogg's Corn Flakes. As Huston writes, it was the most delicious meal of her life![9]

There are bound to be times when the going is difficult and frustration occurs because of a communication problem, an unkind remark by an adult or a child, a bad grade in the weaker language, and so on, and it is crucial that bilingual children receive encouragement and assistance. As they grow older, they must be able to talk with others about what it means to be bilingual and bicultural and express some of the difficulties they may be having.

For school-age children the difficulties may include reading and writing problems in school. Depending on the country and the culture, literacy skills have greater or lesser importance in the curriculum, and bilingual children and adolescents may need additional support in these areas. French schools, for example, put a lot of emphasis on correct spelling and grammar, and bilingual children who are in the process of learning French are often penalized for the errors they make. It is here that parents and other caretakers may be able to explain the situation to bilingual youngsters and help them meet their new challenge. In addition, a few words with a teacher can do wonders. Of course, this is easier if parents have mastered the language themselves and are used to interacting with the school; if that is not the case, some intermediary who is close to the family may be able to step in.

Becoming bilingual and bicultural should be a joyful journey into languages and cultures. When children undertake it, it is important that they be accompanied, if at all possible, by caring and informed adults who will ease their passage from one stage to the next, and with whom they can talk about what they are experiencing. When they have that kind of support, there is every chance that the bilingualism and biculturalism attained will be a success.

18

Effects of Bilingualism on Children

I sometimes receive e-mails or phone calls from young parents who would like their child to become bilingual but are worried that there might be harmful consequences. Many have heard the following:

Myth: Bilingualism has negative effects on the development of children.

I reassure those I interact with, but it is true that because of this view, which is still present in certain circles and countries, some parents hesitate to raise their children to be bilingual, while others worry about the linguistic and cognitive development of their bilingual children. In looking at past studies that established the myth, as well as later studies that came out with the opposite results, we will see that much of the work contained methodological and subject-selection problems. From where we stand today, it is clear that there is no basis for the myth of negative effects—not even with bilingual children who have language disorders.

Problems with Past Studies

Back in 1890, the educator and linguist Simon S. Laurie wrote the following very negative assessment of bilingual children:

> If it were possible for a child or boy to live in two languages at once equally well, so much the worse. His intellectual and spiritual growth would not thereby be doubled but halved. Unity of mind and of character would have great difficulty in asserting itself in such circumstances.[1]

Some thirty years later, the great linguist Otto Jespersen added:

> The brain effort required to master two languages instead of one certainly diminishes the child's power of learning other things which might and ought to be learnt.[2]

During the first half of the twentieth century, many studies seemed to confirm these dire assessments. One such study found that Welsh-English bilingual children had lower IQ scores than monolingual children, and that this inferiority became greater with each year from age seven to age eleven. Another study found that children with those same languages (Welsh and English) were outperformed by monolingual English children in both verbal and nonverbal intelligence tests. And a third study revealed that bilingual Italian-American children were surpassed in measures of mental age by monolingual English-speaking children.[3] In sum, much of the work done at the time found that bilingualism had a negative effect on the child's linguistic, cognitive, and educational development; only a few showed no effect or a positive effect.

It is no wonder, therefore, that parents who had the choice hesitated to raise their children to be bilingual, or quite simply decided not to do so. Einar Haugen, the famous expert on bilingualism, who was himself brought up bilingual in Norwegian and English, had this to say about his parents' tenacity despite such negative opinions:

> I have been a bilingual as far back as I can remember, but it was not until I began reading the literature on the subject that I realized what this meant. Without knowing it, I had been exposed to untold dangers of retardation, intellectual impoverishment, schizophrenia, anomie, and alienation, most of which I had apparently escaped, if only by a hair's breadth. If my parents knew about these dangers, they firmly dismissed them and made me bilingual willy-nilly.[4]

Midway through the last century, the tide turned rather suddenly and many researchers found that bilingualism was, after all, a real asset for the child. A major study conducted by Elizabeth Peal and Wallace Lambert is representative of the research in this period. Peal and Lambert selected a group of ten-year-old children from six French Canadian schools in Montreal and compared the French-English bilinguals with the French monolinguals on a battery of tests. The bilinguals got higher scores on both verbal and nonverbal IQ tests. Subtests showed that the bilinguals had more diversified structures of intelligence and more flexibility in thought—that is, greater cognitive flexibility, greater creativity, and greater divergent thought. In addition, the bilingual students were ahead in content work at school, and their attitudes toward English Canadians were more favorable than those of their monolingual French counterparts.[5] A few years later, Merrill Swain and Jim Cummins conducted a review of studies that had been done. They came to the conclusion that bilinguals are more sensitive to semantic relations between words, are more advanced in understanding the arbitrary assignment of names to referents, are better able to treat sentence structure analytically, are better at restructuring a perceptual situation, have greater social sensitivity and a greater ability to react more flexibly to cognitive feedback, are better at rule-discovery tasks, and have more divergent thinking.[6]

How can one explain such a discrepancy between the research findings from the first part of the twentieth century and those from the second part? And what can parents and others involved with bilingual children take away from all of this? We now know that one of the main problems with interpreting the findings of both the negative and positive studies lies in making sure that the study groups (bilinguals and monolinguals) were truly comparable in every aspect, apart from their bilingualism or monolingualism. The early studies, which often involved IQ and which had found lower IQ scores for bilinguals, had not sufficiently controlled for differences in participants' sex, age, socioeconomic background, and educational opportunities. In addition, it is unclear how the researchers chose their bilingual subjects and if the latter had sufficient command of the language in which they were tested. If they did not, it would be no surprise that they did less well, since most tests, including IQ tests, require a good understanding of the language being used.

Even though the studies from the second half of the twentieth century controlled for these factors more carefully, a bias may

have favored bilingual subjects at the time (recall that later results were in favor of bilinguals). G. MacNab mentions two problems with the Peal and Lambert study. First, the bilingual students
may have come from families more open to different cultures and
more willing to try new experiences; in addition, they may have
been "sharper" students from the start. The second problem pertains to the way students were chosen to be part of the bilingual
group. Peal and Lambert had a very strict criterion: their subjects
had to be balanced bilinguals—that is, equally good in the two languages. Thus, they filtered out many subjects and kept "the best." It
is not surprising, therefore, that the group did so well.[7]

Swain and Cummins themselves pointed out in their 1979 study
that positive findings were usually associated with children who
belonged to the majority-language group and who took part in
language-immersion programs, whereas negative findings were
found with minority-language students whose bilingualism was
not valued and who did not live in a social environment that in-
duced learning.[8] When I finished my own review of the literature on
the effects of bilingualism at the beginning of the 1980s for my
book *Life with Two Languages*, I proposed that bilingualism as such
had no major effect—positive or negative—on the cognitive and intellectual development of children. I cited the applied linguist Barry
McLaughlin, who wrote that the findings of research on the effects
were either contradicted by other research or could be questioned
on methodological grounds. The one conclusion that he accepted
was that having command of a second language makes a difference
if a child is tested in that language. If he or she knows the language
well, the results will be favorable; if not, the results will be less favorable—"a not very surprising finding," McLaughlin noted.[9]

Where Do We Stand Today?

When I started preparing this new book, I was interested in finding out where the effects literature had taken us. I contacted the best-known authority in the field, the Canadian developmental psycholinguist Ellen Bialystok, and she very kindly brought me up to date and sent me recent papers to read.[10] At present, the findings are not as black and white as earlier research—either totally positive or totally negative—seemed to show, and the differences between bilinguals and monolinguals, when any are found, are often specific to a particular task and sometimes rather subtle.

Bialystok has shown repeatedly that bilingualism enhances problem solving where solutions depend heavily on control of attention (she talks of "selective attention" and "inhibitory control") because the task includes misleading information. For example, in a study she conducted with Lili Senman, they presented various objects to monolingual and bilingual children who were between the ages of four and five years old. One object was a sponge that looked like a rock (they called this a rock-sponge). They placed the object on a table and told the children, "Look what I have. Can you tell me what this is?" Most of the children answered correctly that it was a rock. The researcher then revealed the hidden property of the object—the fact that it was a sponge—and asked further questions. There were appearance questions (for example, "What did you think this was when you first saw it?") and a reality question, "What is it really?" This last question was the hardest for children (the answer, of course, was "a sponge"), because the object's perceptual features (it looked like a rock) had to be ignored or inhibited. What Bialystok and Senman found was that monolingual and bilingual children performed similarly on appearance questions but that bilingual children scored reliably better than monolinguals on reality questions. The authors explained this difference by suggesting that bilingual children are more advanced than monolingual children in developing inhibitory control.[11]

Earlier in the book, I discussed another study by Ellen Bialystok and her collaborators that showed that this advantage continues throughout the bilingual's lifespan and is even present in elderly bilinguals.[12] Based on their research, it seems that the processes that manipulate attention to one language or the other, or to both, during language use in bilinguals may be the same cognitive functions that are responsible for managing attention to any set of systems or stimuli, as in Bialystok's studies.

Another domain that has been studied quite extensively in bilingual children, and that is halfway between cognition and language, concerns metalinguistic abilities. These deal with our capacity to analyze different aspects of language (sounds, words, syntax, meaning in words and sentences, and so on) and, if needed, to access and talk about these properties. Psycholinguists have developed numerous metalinguistic tasks that involve different processes. Bialystok differentiates between two such processes, the analysis of representational structures and the control of selective attention; she finds differences between monolinguals and bilinguals for the latter, selective attention (as seen in the study described above), but not for the former.[13] Let me address these processes one at a time.

The first process, analysis of representation, is the ability to construct mental representations with more detail and structure than were part of one's initial implicit knowledge. This process is involved when explaining grammatical errors in a sentence, or substituting one phoneme for another, as when one takes the first sound away from the word "cat" and puts in its place the first sound of the word "mop," to give the word "mat." In these kinds of tasks, monolingual children and bilingual children obtain similar results.

The second process, the control of selective attention, is responsible for directing attention to specific aspects of a stimulus or a mental representation, as we have already seen above. Bialystok tells us that there is a need for such control when a problem contains a conflict or an ambiguity. Arriving at the correct solution demands that children (and adults) attend to one of two possible representations while they inhibit or resist attention to the other. Here are a few examples of tasks given to children that involve control of selective attention: counting words in a correct sentence; using a new (or made-up) name for an object in a sentence (for example, replacing "plane" with "wood" in the sentence "the plane is flying past"); and judging that a sentence, such as "apples grow on noses," is syntactically grammatical even though it contains a semantic anomaly. Ellen Bialystok states that bilingual children do better than their monolingual counterparts on these types of tasks.[14]

In addition to these cognitive and metalinguistic tasks, some linguistic tests, notably vocabulary tests, have also been used in studies comparing bilingual and monolingual children. (Note that other linguistic aspects of bilingualism, such as language dominance, language "mixing," interferences, language choice, and code-switching, have already been covered in Chapter 16.) When vocabulary knowledge is evaluated in children, it is often through receptive vocabulary tests in which they have to choose one picture, among others, that illustrates the words spoken by the experimenter. Ellen Bialystok and her colleague Xiaojia Feng reviewed a number of studies that used such tests and found that bilinguals do less well on this task than monolinguals. This is because the vocabulary they have in each language is often smaller than that of comparable monolinguals. Of course when bilingual children are evaluated in terms of both their languages, then the situation improves greatly, but if one looks at just one language at a time, there is frequently a difference.[15] This is not surprising, however, as bilingual children are starting to be affected by the complementarity principle, which states that bilinguals usually acquire and use their languages for different purposes, in different domains of life, with different people, because different aspects of their life often require different languages. Unfortunately, vocabulary tests do not take this principle into account and hence test results penalize bilingual children. Nevertheless, the authors show that in other language tasks, especially those involving memory, there are no differences between monolinguals and bilinguals.

Bialystok and Feng summarize recent research on the effects of bilingualism on the cognitive development of bilingual children in the following way:

> The picture emerging from these studies is a complex
> portrait of interactions between bilingualism and skill ac-
> quisition in which there are sometimes benefits for bilin-
> gual children, sometimes deficits, and sometimes no con-
> sequence at all.[16]

This is a fair description of what is becoming a complex picture of the often subtle differences between monolingual and bilingual children—when differences exist.

Bilingual Children and Language Disorders

Linguist and speech therapist Susanne Döpke reminds us that some 10 percent of children can be expected to have difficulties with language development. She stresses that this percentage is the *same* for monolingual and bilingual children. The reasons for language delays and language disorders are many, but bilingualism is not one of them, she stresses. Döpke states that a number of conditions in the child's stronger language may signal a language disorder. Among these, we find the inability to understand familiar words or to follow instructions appropriate for the child's age, difficulty in saying or learning words or phrases, the use of language in a strange way, a delay in other areas of development, various behavioral problems, and so on. Döpke insists that discontinuing the home language does not improve the bilingual child's abilities in the majority (school) language; on the contrary, it can have other consequences that can be prejudicial to the child and to his or her environment. Hence, if a child is being raised bilingual, no change should be made in the languages used, despite the widespread and erroneous idea, still conveyed by some professionals, that the child's language disorder will get better if parents revert to just one language. As Döpke states clearly,

> Bilingualism does not cause any type of language disorder and retracting to just one language does not improve a language disorder.[17]

Not only are bilingual children with language disorders not more numerous than monolingual children, but their difficulties are often the same as the latter group's. Psycholinguist Johanne Paradis and her colleagues studied the errors made by seven-year-old bilingual and monolingual children with a disorder called specific language impairment (SLI) and found the same deficit patterns in the two groups. Children with SLI have normal social and emotional development, as well as normal sensory and motor abilities, but their language abilities are below age expectations. They are intelligent and healthy in every way except for the difficulties they have with language. The study examined the tense errors made by these children (for example, "The teddy *want* juice" or "Brendan *bake* a cake last night") and found that the dual language knowledge of the bilingual children with SLI did not cause them to have different patterns of errors from those of their monolingual peers with SLI. The authors concluded that bilingual language learning does not appear to interfere with the overall course of language acquisition, even under conditions of impairment.[18] In a later publication, Paradis states that her group's research finds no empirical support for advising parents to give up speaking one of their two languages to a child who has SLI (especially when the child is acquiring two languages simultaneously).[19]

19

Education and Bilingualism

When the terms "education" and "bilingualism" are put together in the same phrase, they bring up a topic that is both vast and often controversial, if not explosive in certain countries. Since this book is about bilingualism, we will approach the topic with a particular slant, which is that, if at all possible, education should help children and adolescents acquire a second or third language while retaining their first language (or languages). In addition, again if possible, education should encourage the active use of those languages. This position is not very different from an objective proposed by the United Nations Educational, Scientific and Cultural Organization (UNESCO) in its 2002 Universal Declaration on Cultural Diversity:

> Encouraging linguistic diversity—while respecting the mother tongue—at all levels of education, wherever possible, and fostering the learning of several languages from the earliest age.[1]

As we will see, in some programs for bilingual children the educational aim is not bilingualism, whereas in others bilingualism is indeed one of the aims. It is important to underline that this chapter is not about bilingual education as it is known in the United States, but about educational approaches that lead either to monolingualism in children or to bilingualism. What really interests me here is how schools can encourage a child or an adolescent to acquire and use new languages as well as retain the language or languages already known.

When the Aim Is Not Bilingualism

Before addressing the central issue of children who enter school with a language that is different from the school's main language (I will call the former the minority language), I should say a few words about the regular second-language learning that takes place in most schools throughout the world. I am thinking here of how British schoolchildren learn German, for example, how the French learn English, how Americans learn Spanish, and so on. In most cases the learning is rather formal; the language is a subject that is taught, like other subjects, at specific times during the school week. It rarely becomes a means of communication and is not a medium used to teach other subjects. Second-language (or foreign-language) teachers—I was one at the start of my career—often make laudable efforts to transform language learning into an enjoyable and lively activity. In addition to more traditional materials, they use Web-based and other audiovisual methods, as well as diverse communicative strategies, to teach the language in question. But miracles simply don't happen when you have classes of up to twenty or thirty students that meet for just a few hours a week. At the end of their schooling, students usually retain some knowledge of the second language learned, but they have little actual use for it unless they find themselves in a communicative context where the language is needed. In sum, many of these students acquire a base on which they could build real language use, and hence bilingualism, if the situation were appropriate and the need arose. But they are not yet bilingual.

One might think, naively, that children and adolescents who come to school knowing another language (usually a minority language) have a head start in becoming bilingual. After all, won't a young Nicaraguan who enters the American school system with little English become, over time, an active bilingual in Spanish and English? Won't a young North African in France become bilingual in Arabic and French, or a young Turk in Germany become bilingual in Turkish (or Kurdish) and German? In many African and Asian countries, bilingualism does indeed develop in children who come from other language backgrounds when they start attending school. But in areas of the world with minority groups that come from immigration, rare is the country that has a deliberate educational policy of allowing minority children to acquire and retain both their native, immigrant language and the majority language, and hence a policy of fostering bilingualism. The reasons for this are many (political, financial, cultural) and are the object of constant debate.

The main approach that schools take is to integrate these children into the mainstream classroom and get them to acquire the majority language as best they can, without paying attention to, or using, their first language. Numerous problems accompany this approach, which some label "submersion" or "sink or swim." If children do not understand or speak the language used in the school, their learning of skills and content matter is slowed down and they fall behind. In addition, they often feel lonely and insecure, especially if they are alone among children who already know the majority language. Their struggle is even harder when the teachers have no knowledge of the minority language and culture in question and there is no one to help them out. Jim Cummins, an authority on the education of minority children, writes that one of the most frustrating experiences for newcomer students is not being able to express their intelligence, their feelings and ideas, even their humor, to teachers and peers. They cannot do so in the language of the school and they are not allowed to do so in their native language.[2] Autobiographies and memoirs of people who have gone through this ordeal are replete with testimonies like the following:

> Although most of the English teachers knew some
> French, they would make absolutely no use of it [to help
> me]. They argued that the "hard way" was the only way to
> learn. My older sister and I were in the same school. Her
> knowledge of English was far better than mine, but she
> was not allowed to help me, and we were forbidden to
> communicate in French.[3]

The well-known Mexican American labor leader and civil rights activist César Chávez had this to say about his experience:

> In class, one of my biggest problems was the language. Of
> course, we bitterly resented not being able to speak Span-
> ish, but they insisted that we had to learn English. They
> said that if we were American, then we should speak the
> language, and if we wanted to speak Spanish, we should
> go back to Mexico.[4]

There are different variants to this majority-language approach. One is to offer special second-language classes (in the United States, these are called English as a second language, or ESL, classes) where the children are taught, often in a rather formal way, the language used as the medium of instruction in the school. Not only is what is learned not always very useful, despite the considerable efforts of dedicated teachers, but in addition the children suffer from the stigma of being pulled out of the regular classroom to attend such classes, and this widens the gap between them and the other children. Here is what a Portuguese-English bilingual once told me about his experience:

> When I first went to school on arrival in the United States, I was put into an English as a Second Language class. This was where all the non- and limited-English-speaking students ended up. We were at least twenty of varying languages and ages. The teacher spoke only in English. She communicated her instructions to the new arrivals through the students who already understood English. Each language group would end up sitting together to be able to get the teacher's instructions and explanation via the students who were able to interpret. I don't think I learned to speak English in that class; what I learned was on the street from the children I played with.[5]

Numerous researchers have stressed how difficult it is for children and adolescents to follow the regular school curriculum while they are in the process of learning the language of instruction. Jim Cummins stresses the fact that minority-language learners have to catch up to a "moving target" in content matters; he notes that majority-language children are not standing still waiting for the other children to reach their level. As time goes by, concepts become more difficult, vocabulary more technical, and grammatical constructions more sophisticated. As we learned in Chapter 15, Cummins estimates that minority-language children require at least five years to catch up to their majority-language peers in literacy-related language skills.[6] The problem is, many become discouraged and fall behind or drop out.

As minority-language children and adolescents struggle with their "new" language, which some will master while others won't, they are also slowly losing their native language, which is not being reinforced and developed at school. The experience of Richard Rodriguez, author of *Hunger of Memory,* is a case in point; he made it through in the sense that he acquired English, but in the process he lost his Spanish, even though he took traditional Spanish classes in high school (by then it was too late):

> I grew up victim to a disabling confusion. As I grew fluent in English, I no longer could speak Spanish with confidence. I continued to understand spoken Spanish. And in high school, I learned how to read and write Spanish. But for many years I could not pronounce it. A powerful guilt blocked my spoken words; an essential glue was missing whenever I'd try to connect words to form sentences.[7]

If the minority language can be used in the first years of school, it not only has important social, cultural, and psychological benefits for children but it also helps them acquire the second language through the transfer of skills from one language to the other. There comes a point, however, when it is too late. Linguist Lily Wong Fillmore tells us about Freddy, a seventeen-year-old "former" English learner who was being tutored in mathematics in order to pass the California High School Exit Examination (he had already failed the math part twice). He lacked the vocabulary and the grammatical resources in English to make sense of the material he read. Wong Fillmore poses the question of whether it would have helped if the tutorial sessions had been conducted in Spanish, Freddy's first language. In his case, it would have helped when he was younger, she says, but, having been schooled exclusively in English, Freddy no longer understood or spoke Spanish as well as he did English. Wong Fillmore concludes that Freddy would have found it easier to learn what he was supposed to be learning in school had he received content instruction in Spanish.[8]

Acknowledging the importance of instruction in the first language, as underlined by the UNESCO objective mentioned at the beginning of this chapter, some educational bodies have established transitional programs during which the student's first language serves as a bridge toward the second, majority language. These types of programs were common in the United States in the second part of the twentieth century and exist now in such countries as The Netherlands, England, and Sweden, according to education expert Maria Brisk.[9] Students are instructed in their first language for a limited period, while they are acquiring language skills in the majority language. As time goes by (programs last anywhere between one and four years, depending on the country), the majority language plays an increasingly important role and eventually takes over completely. The advantages of these programs are many: children start school in a language that they understand and that is linked to their home culture, they can interact easily with the teacher and the other children, they make headway in content subjects as they are acquiring the majority language, the literacy skills they acquire can be transferred to their new language, and so on. The one problem, in terms of bilingualism, is that the programs are by nature transitional and no effort is made after they are over to maintain the children's native language and culture. Some children may get sufficient help from their home and community to hold on to their first language, but many others will assimilate into the mainstream culture and lose their linguistic and cultural roots. They will go from being monolingual in a minority language to being basically monolingual in the majority language. For many, bilingualism will have been experienced only during the short transition period between the two.

When the Aim Is Bilingualism

Before discussing examples of how schools can help children become, and remain, bilingual, let's consider some recent history.[10] Back in the 1960s, a very important educational innovation took place in the small town of St. Lambert in Quebec, Canada. It would have repercussions around the world, and its effects have grown stronger year after year. Some English Canadian parents living in the predominantly French-speaking town were dissatisfied with the traditional manner in which French was taught in school. With the help of educators and psychologists from McGill University (Wallace Lambert, Richard Tucker, and others), they set up an "immersion program" in which English-speaking children were taught in French, by French-speaking teachers, starting in kindergarten. The children were allowed to speak English with one another in kindergarten, but in grade one this was discouraged. From first grade on, the teachers never spoke English to the students or with one another, so as to create, so far as possible, a totally French-speaking environment. The children were taught to read and write in French starting in grade one. In grade two, they started having English-language classes for about an hour a day, but the rest of the program was in French. In the following grades more English was brought in, so that by grade six, more than half of the teaching was in English. In this way, the children were first taught in a second language and then, little by little, their first language was introduced as a second medium of instruction.

At first sight, one might think this was just another form of the submersion program discussed in the first section of this chapter. In reality, however, the differences were many. All children in the classroom were from the same language background, their home language was respected and it was introduced as a medium of instruction relatively soon, their parents were supportive of the program, and the teachers had high expectations for the children's achievement. And, indeed, the approach proved to be very successful. By grade six, the children were in no way behind control groups in English-language skills and in content subjects (they had transferred their newly acquired reading skills from French to English), their level of intelligence was equivalent to that of the controls, and their knowledge of French was far better than that of other English Canadians their age. And, most important, they had learned a language by using it in context instead of by acquiring it through formal instruction. French now covered a few domains of their life, even if English remained the dominant language. The one thing missing was the use of French outside the school, but this was left to the families to work on. The success of the St. Lambert project led to the development of similar programs in Canada, the United States, and many other countries, modeled on the original format or some variant of it. Late-immersion or language-switch programs, for example, start the instruction in the second language in later grades; partial-immersion programs use the second language for half of the day or for only certain subjects, and so on.

The immersion approach has been used with children from dominant language groups, such as English-speaking children in English Canada, but also with minority children. Let me mention one such example involving a Navajo language-revival program in Fort Defiance, Arizona. On the basis of work by the linguist Michael Krauss, Teresa McCarty, an education specialist, reminds us that America's indigenous languages are in dire danger of being lost: of the 175 languages currently found in the United States, only 20 are naturally acquired by children.[11] Navajo is the most-used Indian language, but it is no longer the primary language for a growing number of Navajo children. Hence a Navajo immersion program was started in 1986 so that children could acquire Navajo while making progress in English and their other subjects. Children in the Fort Defiance Elementary School started with Navajo and were taught reading and writing skills in that language before moving on to English. In the lower grades all communication occurred in Navajo, but the teachers were bilingual and could help them when they had difficulties. As the children moved up the grades, English was brought in more and more (half a day for each language in grades two and three, for example). What is striking about the program is that Navajo caretakers spent time speaking with children in Navajo in the evening, after school, and they took part in activities with the students, such as bookmaking. An assessment that was done in fourth grade was most favorable in terms of the students' Navajo- and English-language skills as well as their performance in subjects such as mathematics. In addition, students had regained pride in being Navajo.[12]

A highly respected educator, Wayne Holm, has been teaching in Navajo schools for some fifty years. Holm stresses the fact that young Navajos who have been through the program now have the choice of continuing to speak and use Navajo in their later life:

> Learning the language of one's people does not force you to live your life in one and only one way. It keeps your options open. As a young adult, you can choose *whether* to use your language, *who* to use your language with, and *what* things you will talk about in your language. Children whose parents or schools deny them access to their language [are deprived] . . . of choice. . . . By the time a teenager or young adult might choose to speak the language, for most, it is already too late.[13]

There is a type of educational program that promotes bilingualism and biliteracy, as well as a very real understanding of the people and cultures involved. It is the dual-language program (also called a two-way program), in which two languages are used throughout schooling and the students come from both language backgrounds. An example of one such program in the United States is the Amigos School, located in Cambridge, Massachusetts. Part of the Cambridge public schools, the Amigos School offers bilingual, biliterate education from kindergarten to eighth grade for students from families in which Spanish is the dominant language, as well as students for whom English is the main language. Every student group, or class, has a balance of native-English and native-Spanish speakers. Groups rotate between their English classroom and their Spanish classroom. For example, kindergarten students spend two and a half days in one language classroom and then switch to the other language classroom for the remainder of the week. Grades one through three rotate weekly between the language classrooms. In later grades, students are exposed daily to both languages when they switch from a subject taught in Spanish to another taught in English. Long-term projects are usually done in just one language. Students use the language appropriate to the classroom or subject; in the public domain, such as in the corridors, at school assemblies, and so on, both languages are used. One unique aspect of this kind of program is that students who are dominant in one language work with, and help, students dominant in the other language. This is education at its best, with both languages and cultures being respected and valued.[14]

I should pause here to say a few words about biliteracy. Many parents and educators wonder whether literacy in one language helps or hinders literacy in the other. In 2006, the National Literacy Panel for Language Minority Children and Youth, a panel of sixteen scholars commissioned by the U.S. Department of Education, released its report after four years of work. The extensive volume includes a section on first- and second-language literacy. What emerges is that there is a real cross-linguistic influence of literacy knowledge, processes, and strategies from one language (predominantly the strongest one) to the other. For example, word-reading skills acquired in one language transfer to the other; in early stages of second-language spelling development, the first-language phonology and graphophonic rules affect the spelling of the second language (when the languages have similar writing systems, of course); and there is also cross-language transfer of reading-comprehension ability.[15] In short, the literacy skills a student has in one language help the student develop literacy skills in the other. Of course, the extent of the facilitation will depend on the relation between the two languages and their writing systems. Facilitation will be greater between Spanish and English, for example, than between Chinese and English. But clearly biliteracy is possible, and it will not hinder the bilingual child.[16]

Another example of a successful dual-language program is found in Switzerland, in the bilingual town of Bienne (its French name), also called Biel (its German name). The high school there offers a three-year dual-language program leading to the high school degree (or Maturité). The program contains both French-speaking and Swiss German–speaking students, with about 50 percent of each per class. Teaching takes place in the teacher's mother tongue (French or German) and subjects are taught in the same language throughout the three years. About half the courses are in German and the other half in French, so that students are using their first language half the time and their second language the other half. Students are regrouped by language only for language courses (for example, German-speaking students take German literature in German). Teachers help the nonnative speakers in their courses by translating from time to time and by making sure that the subject matter is understood. When marking papers, they are not excessively strict when students make errors in their weaker language. Students who follow a subject in their native language are coached in how to help their nonnative-speaking fellow students; they can answer their questions, translate from time to time, and so on. The program is organized so that all students find themselves in a helping role half the time and in an assisted role the other half. They are encouraged to interact with one another across language groups during breaks, lunchtime, and extracurricular activities such as sports, camps, concerts, and study trips. This allows the Swiss Germans to improve their French and the Swiss French students to do the same with German as well as Swiss German (the everyday language used in the German part of Switzerland).

The Amigos and the Biel/Bienne programs are exceptions, unfortunately. According to the Center for Applied Linguistics, in Washington, D.C., there were some 332 dual-language bilingual programs of this type in elementary schools in the United States in 2008, which represents only about 1 percent of all programs. But, just like the early immersion programs, they are establishing a model for what can be done to help students acquire two languages, discover the culture of the other language group, interact with speakers of that language and culture, and have a better understanding of what it means to be able to help someone else who does not understand what is being said and to be helped by someone when you are in the same situation. For all of those who have lived through the sink or swim approach in education (I was one of those children), these kinds of programs are extremely promising. They reconcile education and bilingualism and benefit all those concerned, whether they come from the dominant culture or from a minority culture.[17]

Conclusion

Some ten months have gone by since I wrote the introduction to this book and I am still marveling at people who are bilingual and bicultural. I saw the baker's wife yesterday when I went to her store, and we spoke French as usual. I wanted to tell her I had just finished a book and that I had mentioned her bilingualism in it, but I decided to wait until it was published. I did tell the car mechanic the other day, though, and he just smiled and moved on to what was wrong with my car. And just this morning I saw the little children from the day care across the street and thought of their songs in French and Italian that I had enjoyed so much.

All this made me realize, yet again, just how natural living with two or more languages really is, but also how bilingualism and biculturalism are still so poorly understood. Although I have tackled in this book some fifteen myths about these phenomena, I am the first to acknowledge that some still have a long life ahead of them. That said, it is worth repeating over and over again that there are probably more bilinguals on the earth today than monolinguals and that, in this age of global communication and travel, the number will surely increase. Bilingualism and biculturalism are therefore normal phenomena, even if in large, strongly monolingual countries they are seen as the exception.

The myths that I would like most to see disappear are those that touch the bilingual most closely, notably the myth that bilinguals have equal and perfect knowledge of their languages (to which many add that they also speak them without an accent), the myth that bilinguals have double or split personalities, and the myth that bilingualism has negative effects on the development of children. Concerning the first, I recall vividly an illustrious Sorbonne professor telling me some two years after I had returned to France, after spending ten years in English schools, "You know, Grosjean, I really wondered whether you would ever be able to know either language correctly." Clearly this professor had a very traditional view of bilingualism and did not understand that, after having reorganized themselves, the languages of a bilingual usually attain the linguistic level needed for the person's new life.

As for the myth concerning double or split personalities, I am reminded of Olivier Todd's autobiography, where he reports that the French philosopher Jean-Paul Sartre told him, as a young man, that his real problem was the fact that he was torn between England and France. The notion that one can be bicultural—with roots in two cultures, a defender of both although possibly dominant in one—was simply not accepted then. When I look around today and see so many bilingual and bicultural people, some in quite visible public positions, still hesitant to acknowledge publicly their other language and culture, I realize that we are not there yet, at least in some parts of the world.

Finally, the myth that bilingualism has negative effects on the development of children reminds me of Einar Haugen, the foremost specialist in bilingualism, whose parents dismissed the "apparent dangers" of bilingualism and made him bilingual all the same. Thank heaven they did, as the world is all the better thanks to his scholarly work in this field.

However, despite the myths I am optimistic. An increasing number of children and adolescents in the process of becoming bilingual, bicultural, and, for some, biliterate *are* receiving the attention they require precisely because they are bilingual and bicultural. As I have said, there are bound to be times when the going is difficult and frustration occurs. It is crucial, therefore, that all receive encouragement and assistance. As bilingual children and adolescents grow older, they must be allowed to talk about what it means to be bilingual and bicultural and to express some of the difficulties they may be having. Caring and informed adults must accompany them (many already do) and ease their passage from one stage to the next. I dream of the moment when these young people and, later, adults will all be proud of their languages and cultures, and be accepted for who they are—bilingual and bicultural individuals, quite simply.

Interested readers can contact the author by means of his Web site: www.francoisgrosjean.ch.

Notes

1. WHY ARE PEOPLE BILINGUAL?

1. Raymond G. Gordon, ed., *Ethnologue: Languages of the World,* 15th ed. (Dallas: SIL International, 2005); www.ethnologue.com.
2. Ibid. William Mackey, *Bilingualism as a World Problem* (Montreal: Harvest House, 1967).
3. From François Grosjean, *Life with Two Languages: An Introduction to Bilingualism* (Cambridge, Mass.: Harvard University Press, 1982), 15.
4. Andrew Buncombe and Tessa MacArthur, "London: Multilingual Capital of the World," *Independent* (London), 29 March 1999; www.phon.ucl.ac.uk/home/estuary/multiling.htm. James Black, "The English Market Town Where They Speak 65 Languages . . . and a Quarter of the People Are Eastern European Migrants," *Daily Mail,* 23 April 2008.
5. From Grosjean, *Life with Two Languages,* 36.
6. Ibid.
7. Ibid.
8. See François Grosjean, "The Bilingualism and Biculturalism of the Deaf," in *Studying Bilinguals* (Oxford: Oxford University Press, 2008), chap. 13.
9. European Commission, *Europeans and Their Languages,* Special Eurobarometer 243 (2006); ec.europa.eu/public_opinion/archives/ebs/ebs_243_en.pdf.

10. 2001 Census of Canada, www12.statcan.ca/english/census01/home/index.cfm.

11. Grosjean, *Life with Two Languages,* 54-57.

12. U.S. Census 2000, www.census.gov/main/www/cen2000.html. One obtains a very similar figure from the U.S. Census Bureau's 2005-2007 American Community Survey (ACS), which is based on sampling (1 out of every 480 households received a questionnaire). In the 2005-2007 survey, a total of 19.5 percent of household members age five years and older reported speaking a language other than English in the household. If one takes away one or two points for those who speak no English at all, the percentage of bilinguals is quite similar to that based on the 2000 census.

13. The figure presented in the 2005-2007 ACS (ibid.) is close to 34 million.

14. From Grosjean, *Life with Two Languages,* 9.

15. Ibid.

2. DESCRIBING BILINGUALS

1. Nancy Huston, *Losing North: Musings on Land, Tongue and Self* (Toronto: McArthur, 2002), 40.

2. Leonard Bloomfield, *Language* (New York: Holt, Rinehart and Winston, 1933), 56.

3. Christophe Thiery, "True Bilingualism and Second Language Learning," in David Gerver and H. Wallace Sinaiko, eds., *Language Interpretation and Communication* (New York: Plenum, 1978), 145-153; quotation on 146.

4. Einar Haugen, *The Norwegian Language in America: A Study in Bilingual Behavior* (Bloomington: Indiana University Press, 1969), 9.

5. Uriel Weinreich, *Languages in Contact* (The Hague: Mouton, 1968). William Mackey, "The Description of Bilingualism," *Canadian Journal of Linguistics* 71 (1962): 51-85.

6. For an example of such a questionnaire, see Ping Li, Sara Sepanski,

and Xiaowei Zhao, "Language History Questionnaire: A Web-Based Interface for Bilingual Research," *Behavioral Research Methods* 38 (2006): 202–210.

3. THE FUNCTIONS OF LANGUAGES

1. For more about Pomerode, see www.pomerodeonline.com.br. For a classic study of the bilingual community there, see Jürgen Heye, "Bilingualism and Language Maintenance in Two Communities in Santa Catarina, Brazil," in William McCormack and Stephen Wurm, eds., *Language and Society* (The Hague: Mouton, 1979), 401–422.

2. On the complementarity principle, see François Grosjean, "The Bilingual Individual," *Interpreting* 2 (1997): 163–187.

3. Quoted in François Grosjean, *Life with Two Languages: An Introduction to Bilingualism* (Cambridge, Mass.: Harvard University Press, 1982), 141.

4. François Grosjean, *Studying Bilinguals* (Oxford: Oxford University Press, 2008), chap. 3.

5. Grosjean, *Life with Two Languages*, 275.

6. Ibid., 276.

7. See, for example, James Flege, Ian MacKay, and Thorsten Piske, "Assessing Bilingual Dominance," *Applied Psycholinguistics* 23 (2002): 567–598.

8. See Ping Li, Sara Sepanski, and Xiaowei Zhao, "Language History Questionnaire: A Web-Based Interface for Bilingual Research," *Behavioral Research Methods* 38 (2006): 202–210.

9. Robert Cooper, "Degree of Bilingualism," in Joshua Fishman, Robert Cooper, and Roxana Ma, eds., *Bilingualism in the Barrio* (Bloomington: Indiana University Press, 1971), 273–309.

10. Viorica Marian and Ulrich Neisser, "Language-Dependent Recall of Autobiographical Memories," *Journal of Experimental Psychology: General* 129 (2000): 361–368.

4. LANGUAGE MODE AND LANGUAGE CHOICE

1. The scientific definition of language mode is the state of activation of the bilingual's languages and language-processing mechanism at a given point in time. I discuss this in several chapters in François Grosjean, *Studying Bilinguals* (Oxford: Oxford University Press, 2008).

2. Carroll Barber, "Trilingualism in an Arizona Yaqui Village," in Paul Turner, ed., *Bilingualism in the Southwest* (Tucson: University of Arizona Press, 1973), 295–318; quotation on 305.

3. I deal extensively with language choice in François Grosjean, *Life with Two Languages: An Introduction to Bilingualism* (Cambridge, Mass.: Harvard University Press, 1982), chap. 3.

4. Joan Rubin, *National Bilingualism in Paraguay* (The Hague: Mouton, 1968).

5. Gerard Hoffman, "Puerto Ricans in New York: A Language-Related Ethnographic Summary," in Joshua Fishman, Robert Cooper, and Roxana Ma, eds., *Bilingualism in the Barrio* (Bloomington: Indiana University Press, 1971), 13–42.

6. Rubin, *National Bilingualism in Paraguay.*

5. CODE-SWITCHING AND BORROWING

1. Example from Lenora Timm, "Code-Switching in *War and Peace,*" in Michel Paradis, ed., *Aspects of Bilingualism* (Columbia, S.C.: Hornbeam, 1978), 236–249.

2. Lynn Haney, *Naked at the Feast: A Biography of Josephine Baker* (London: Robson, 1995), 201.

3. Einar Haugen, *The Norwegian Language in America: A Study in Bilingual Behavior* (Bloomington: Indiana University Press, 1969), 70.

4. François Grosjean, *Life with Two Languages: An Introduction to Bilingualism* (Cambridge, Mass.: Harvard University Press, 1982), 150.

5. Ibid., 115.

6. Carol Scotton and William Ury, "Bilingual Strategies: The Social Functions of Code-Switching," *Linguistics* 193 (1977): 5–20.

7. Paul Preston, *Mother Father Deaf* (Cambridge, Mass.: Harvard University Press, 1995), 134.

8. See the work of researchers such as Peter Auer, Penelope Gardner-Chloros, Carol Myers-Scotton, Pieter Muysken, Shana Poplack, and Jeanine Treffers-Daller.

9. Shana Poplack, "Sometimes I'll Start a Sentence in Spanish y Termino en Español: Toward a Typology of Code-Switching," *Linguistics* 18 (1980): 581–618; quotation on 615–616.

10. See François Grosjean, *Studying Bilinguals* (Oxford: Oxford University Press, 2008).

11. Examples from Carol Pfaff, "Constraints on Language Mixing: Intrasentential Code-Switching and Borrowing in Spanish/English," *Language* 55 (1979): 291–318.

12. Example from Anthony Lozano, "Tracing the Spanish Language," *Agenda* 10 (1980): 32–38.

13. Example from Wendy Redlinger, "A Description of Transference and Code-Switching in Mexican-American English and Spanish," in Gary Keller, Richard Teschner, and Silva Viera, eds., *Bilingualism in the Bicentennial and Beyond* (New York: Bilingual Press/Editorial Bilingüe, 1976), 41–52.

14. Uriel Weinreich, *Languages in Contact* (The Hague: Mouton, 1968), 57.

15. Ibid.

16. As quoted in Otto Jespersen, *Growth and Structure of the English Language* (New York: Appleton-Century, 1923), 94.

6. SPEAKING AND WRITING MONOLINGUALLY

1. Quoted in Carroll Barber, "Trilingualism in an Arizona Yaqui Village," in Paul Turner, ed., *Bilingualism in the Southwest* (Tucson: University of Arizona Press, 1973), 305.

2. Olivier Todd, *Carte d'identités* (Paris: Plon, 2005).

3. David Green, "Mental Control of the Bilingual Lexico-Semantic System," *Bilingualism: Language and Cognition* 1 (1998): 67–81. François Grosjean, "The Bilingual's Language Modes," in Janet Nicol, ed., *One Mind, Two Languages: Bilingual Language Processing* (Oxford: Blackwell, 2001), 1–22.

4. Jubin Abutalebi and David Green, "Control Mechanisms in Bilingual Language Production: Neural Evidence from Language Switching Studies," *Language and Cognitive Processes* 23 (2008): 557–582.

5. In François Grosjean, "An Attempt to Isolate, and Then Differentiate, Transfer and Interference," *International Journal of Bilingualism* (forthcoming), I suggest that we use the term "transfer" for static phenomena and the term "interference" for dynamic phenomena. I also propose a way of differentiating empirically between the two.

6. Example from Einar Haugen, *The Norwegian Language in America: A Study in Bilingual Behavior* (Bloomington: Indiana University Press, 1969).

7. Nancy Huston, *Losing North: Musings on Land, Tongue and Self* (Toronto: McArthur, 2002), 41.

8. Example from Ronald Sheen, "The Importance of Negative Transfer in the Speech of Near Bilinguals," *International Review of Applied Linguistics* 18 (1980): 105–119.

9. Examples from William Mackey, *Bilinguisme et contact des langues* (Paris: Editions Klincksiek, 1976).

10. Uriel Weinreich, *Languages in Contact* (The Hague: Mouton, 1968).

11. Paul Preston, *Mother Father Deaf* (Cambridge, Mass.: Harvard University Press), 136–137. An experimental study by researchers Jennie Pyers and Karen Emmorey showed that bilinguals reduced the number of times they furrowed their eyebrows when they switched from a bilingual to a monolingual mode, but they did not stop completely; the facial cue still occurred one-third of the time when

ASL-bilingual speakers asked what-where-who-which questions in English of monolingual English speakers. See Pyers and Emmorey, "The Face of Bimodal Bilingualism: Grammatical Markers in American Sign Language Are Produced When Bilinguals Speak to English Monolinguals," *Psychological Science* 19 (2008): 531-535.

12. Huston, *Losing North*, 27.

13. See, for example, Vivian Cook, *Effects of the Second Language on the First* (Clevedon, U.K.: Multilingual Matters, 2003).

14. Eva Hoffman, *Lost in Translation* (New York: Penguin, 1989), 273.

15. See, for example, François Grosjean, "The Bilingual as a Competent but Specific Speaker-Hearer," *Journal of Multilingual and Multicultural Development* 6 (1985): 467-477.

16. Vivian Cook makes a similar argument. See, for instance, Cook, "Evidence for Multicompetence," *Language Learning* 42 (1992): 557-591.

7. HAVING AN ACCENT IN A LANGUAGE

1. James Flege, "Factors Affecting Degree of Perceived Foreign Accent in English," *Journal of the Acoustical Society of America* 84 (1988): 70-79.

2. Theo Bongaerts, Brigitte Planken, and Erik Schils, "Can Late Starters Attain a Native Accent in a Foreign Language? A Test of the Critical Period," in David Singleton and Zsolt Lengyel, eds., *The Age Factor in Second Language Acquisition* (Clevedon, U.K.: Multilingual Matters, 1995), 30-50.

3. Eva Hoffman, *Lost in Translation* (New York: Penguin, 1989), 122.

4. James Bossard, "The Bilingual as a Person: Linguistic Identification with Status," *American Sociological Review* 10: 699-709; quotation on 705.

5. Nancy Huston and Leila Sebba, *Lettres parisiennes* (Paris: Editions J'ai Lu, 2006), 13.

6. Nancy Huston, *Losing North: Musings on Land, Tongue and Self* (Toronto: McArthur, 2002), 25.

7. Elizabeth K. Beaujour, *Alien Tongues: Bilingual Writers of the "First" Emigration* (Ithaca, N.Y.: Cornell University Press, 1989), 73.

8. An anonymous reviewer kindly reminded me of this aspect.

8. LANGUAGES ACROSS THE LIFESPAN

1. Linda Galloway, "Language Impairment and Recovery in Polyglot Aphasia: A Case Study of a Hepta-Lingual," in Michel Paradis, ed., *Aspects of Bilingualism* (Columbia, S.C.: Hornbeam, 1978), 121–130.

2. Nancy Huston and Leila Sebba, *Lettres parisiennes* (Paris: Editions J'ai Lu, 2006), 76.

3. Nancy Huston, *Losing North: Musings on Land, Tongue and Self* (Toronto: McArthur, 2002), 43.

4. See, for example, Robert Schrauf, "Bilingualism and Aging," in Jeanette Altarriba and Roberto Heredia, eds., *An Introduction to Bilingualism: Principles and Processes* (New York: Lawrence Erlbaum, 2007), 105–127.

5. Ellen Bialystok, Michelle Martin, and Mythili Viswanathan, "Bilingualism across the Lifespan: The Rise and Fall of Inhibitory Control," *International Journal of Bilingualism* 9 (2005): 103–119.

6. Ellen Bialystok, Fergus Craik, and Morris Freedman, "Bilingualism as a Protection against the Onset of Symptoms of Dementia," *Neuropsychologia* 45 (2007): 459–464.

9. ATTITUDES AND FEELINGS ABOUT BILINGUALISM

1. Unless otherwise indicated, the testimonies in this chapter are taken from François Grosjean, *Life with Two Languages: An Introduction to Bilingualism* (Cambridge, Mass.: Harvard University Press, 1982).

2. Much of this discussion is based on two research surveys, one conducted by Veroboj Vildomec—see Vildomec, *Multilingualism* (Leiden: A. W. Sythoff, 1963)—and the other by me, with results published in Grosjean, *Life with Two Languages.* In addition, I will use the results of a large public survey: European Commission, *Europeans*

and Their Languages, Special Eurobarometer 243 (2006);
ec.europa.eu/public_opinion/archives/ebs/ebs_243_en.pdf.

3. *Daily Telegraph,* 6 February 2008, online at telegraph.co.uk; BBC,
14 December 2007, http://news.bbc.co.uk/sport2/hi/football/
international/7137847.stm.

4. Anatoliy Kharkhurin, "The Effect of Linguistic Proficiency, Age of
Second Language Acquisition, and Length of Exposure to a New
Cultural Environment on Bilinguals' Divergent Thinking," *Bilingualism: Language and Cognition* 11 (2008): 225–243.

5. European Commission, *Europeans and Their Languages.*

6. Ibid., 1.

7. Based on Grosjean, *Life with Two Languages.*

8. Richard Rodriguez, *Hunger of Memory: The Education of Richard Rodriguez* (New York: Bantam, 1983), 24–25.

9. Paul Preston, *Mother Father Deaf* (Cambridge, Mass.: Harvard University Press, 1995), 147.

10. Einar Haugen, "The Stigmata of Bilingualism," in Anwar Dil, ed.,
The Ecology of Language: Essays by Einar Haugen (Stanford: Stanford
University Press, 1972), 307–324; quotation on 308.

11. Barry McLaughlin, *Second-Language Acquisition in Childhood* (Hillsdale, N.J.: Lawrence Erlbaum, 1978), 2–3.

12. Aneta Pavlenko, *Emotions and Multilingualism* (Cambridge: Cambridge University Press, 2005), 23.

10. BILINGUALS WHO ARE ALSO BICULTURAL

1. Biculturalism has been studied much less than bilingualism, and
very few definitions of it are offered in the literature. In Angela-
MinhTu Nguyen and Verónica Benet-Martínez, "Biculturalism Unpacked: Components, Measurement, Individual Differences, and
Outcomes," *Social and Personality Psychology Compass* 1 (2007): 101–
114, the authors describe bicultural individuals as those who have
been exposed to two cultures and have internalized them. They
add that biculturalism also entails the synthesis of cultural norms

from two groups into one behavioral repertoire, or the ability to switch between cultural schemas, norms, and behaviors in response to cultural cues. Thus, their description includes the three characteristics that I have given here.

2. From François Grosjean, *Life with Two Languages: An Introduction to Bilingualism* (Cambridge, Mass.: Harvard University Press, 1982), 166.

3. Nancy Huston, *Losing North: Musings on Land, Tongue and Self* (Toronto: McArthur, 2002), 70–71.

4. Paul Preston, *Mother Father Deaf* (Cambridge, Mass.: Harvard University Press, 1995), 136.

5. Grosjean, *Life with Two Languages,* 159.

6. Personal communication.

7. To simplify things, I will refer to biculturals as having just two cultures from now on, but everything said also applies to people who belong to a greater number of cultures.

8. John Berry, a social psychologist, uses the following labels for the four possibilities mentioned here, respectively: assimilation, separation, marginalization, and integration. See, for example, John Berry, "Integration: A Psychological and Cultural Perspective," paper presented at the conference Conceptualising Integration, organized by the Estonian Integration Foundation, Tallinn, Estonia, 18–19 October 2007. One problem is that these labels are based on immigration and the ensuing acculturation, whereas people can and do become bicultural without actually moving from one country to another.

9. Preston, *Mother Father Deaf,* 199.

10. Olivier Todd, *Carte d'identités* (Paris: Plon, 2005), my translation.

11. Veronica Chambers, "The Secret Latina," *Essence,* July 2000; www.veronicachambers.com/secret.html.

12. Teresa LaFromboise, Hardin Coleman, and Jennifer Gerton, "Psychological Impact of Biculturalism: Evidence and Theory," *Psychological Bulletin* 114 (1993): 395–412.

13. Preston, *Mother Father Deaf,* 228.

11. PERSONALITY, THINKING AND DREAMING, AND EMOTIONS IN BILINGUALS

1. ReutersLife newswire, "Switching Languages Can Also Switch Personality: Study," 24 June 2008; www.reuters.com/article/lifestyleMolt/idUSSP4652020080624.

2. Unless otherwise indicated, the testimonies in this chapter are taken from François Grosjean, *Life with Two Languages: An Introduction to Bilingualism* (Cambridge, Mass.: Harvard University Press, 1982).

3. Robert Di Pietro, "Code-Switching as a Verbal Strategy among Bilinguals," in Fred Eckman, ed., *Current Themes in Linguistics: Bilingualism, Experimental Linguistics, and Language Typologies* (Washington, D.C.: Hemisphere Publishing, 1977), 3–13.

4. Charles Gallagher, "North African Problems and Prospects: Language and Identity," in Joshua Fishman, Charles Ferguson, and Jyotirindra Das Gupta, eds., *Language Problems in Developing Nations* (New York: Wiley, 1968), 129–150.

5. Susan Ervin, "Language and TAT Content in Bilinguals," *Journal of Abnormal and Social Psychology* 68 (1964): 500–507.

6. Susan Ervin, "An Analysis of the Interaction of Language, Topic, and Listener," in John Gumperz and Dell Hymes, eds., *The Ethnography of Communication,* special issue of *American Anthropologist* 66, Part 2 (1964): 86–102.

7. David Luna, Torsten Ringberg, and Laura Peracchio, "One Individual, Two Identities: Frame Switching among Biculturals," *Journal of Consumer Research* 35 (2008): 279–293.

8. Grosjean, *Life with Two Languages.*

9. Ervin, "Language and TAT Content," 506.

10. Grosjean, *Life with Two Languages.*

11. Personal communication. Aneta Pavlenko is currently doing research on these issues. I wish to thank her for discussing them with me.

12. Veroboj Vildomec, *Multilingualism* (Leiden: A. W. Sythoff, 1963).

13. Aneta Pavlenko, *Emotions and Multilingualism* (Cambridge: Cambridge University Press, 2005), 227.

14. Aneta Pavlenko, "Bilingualism and Emotions," *Multilingua* 21 (2002): 45–78.

15. Monika Schmid, *First Language Attrition, Use and Maintenance: The Case of German Jews in Anglophone Countries* (Amsterdam: John Benjamins, 2002).

16. Nancy Huston and Leila Sebba, *Lettres parisiennes* (Paris: Editions J'ai Lu, 2006).

17. Nancy Huston, *Losing North: Musings on Land, Tongue and Self* (Toronto: McArthur, 2002), 49–50.

18. Pavlenko, *Emotions and Multilingualism*, 147.

19. Paul Preston, *Mother Father Deaf* (Cambridge, Mass.: Harvard University Press, 1995), 136.

20. Huston and Sebba, *Lettres parisiennes*, 138.

21. Pavlenko, *Emotions and Multilingualism*, 22–23.

12. BILINGUAL WRITERS

1. Frederick R. Karl, *Joseph Conrad* (New York: Farrar, Straus and Giroux, 1979), quotation on 697.

2. With one or two exceptions I give book titles in English, for readers' convenience. Other out-of-the-ordinary authors who write fiction in their second or third language include André Aciman, Ha Jin, Andreï Makine, Dai Sijie, Ahdaf Soueif, and Xu Xi. I owe this information to Elizabeth Beaujour (who was a great help when I was preparing this chapter), as well as to an anonymous reviewer.

3. Elizabeth Beaujour, *Alien Tongues: Bilingual Russian Writers of the "First" Emigration* (Ithaca, N.Y.: Cornell University Press, 1989), 174. Another book that is often cited on this subject is Steven G. Kellman, *The Translingual Imagination* (Lincoln: University of Nebraska Press, 2000).

4. Beaujour, *Alien Tongues,* 52, 62.

5. Ariel Dorfman, "Footnotes to a Double Life," in Wendy Lesser, ed., *The Genius of Language: Fifteen Writers Reflect on Their Mother Tongues* (New York: Pantheon, 2004), 208.

6. Beaujour, *Alien Tongues,* 64, 114.

7. Ibid., 66, 95.

8. Jane Sullivan (interview with Nancy Huston), "The Trouble with Cultural Dislocation," *Sydney Morning Herald,* 22 September 2007; www.SMH.com.au/news/books/the-trouble-with-cultural-dislocation.

9. Nancy Huston, *Losing North: Musings on Land, Tongue and Self* (Toronto: McArthur, 2002), 37–38.

10. Gerry Feehily, "Biography—Nancy Huston: A View from Both Sides," *Independent,* 22 February 2008; www.independent.co.uk/arts-entertainment/books/features/biography--nancy-huston.

11. Sullivan (interview with Huston), "The Trouble with Cultural Dislocation." Huston, *Losing North,* 39.

12. Beaujour, *Alien Tongues,* 111.

13. Quoted from Junot Díaz, "The Brief Wondrous Life of Oscar Wao," *New Yorker,* 25 December 2000, an excerpt from the book, available online at www.newyorker.com/archive; see also Junot Díaz, *The Brief Wondrous Life of Oscar Wao* (New York: Riverhead Books, 2007), 17.

14. Susana Chávez-Silverman, "Flora y Fauna Crónica," in *Killer Crónicas: Bilingual Memories* (Madison: University of Wisconsin Press, 2004), 5.

15. In addition to the authors mentioned already, several others have written, or write, in their two or more languages, including: André Brink (Afrikaans, English), Ariel Dorfman (Spanish, English), Claude Esteban (Spanish, French), Romain Gary (French, English), Julien Green (French, English), Milan Kundera (Czech, French), Jonathan Littell (English, French), John Milton (Latin, Greek, Italian, English). My thanks to Elizabeth Beaujour for supplying much of this information, and also to John K. Hale for the infor-

mation on John Milton. Beaujour's remark about bilingual writers is taken from the syllabus for Professor Beaujour's City University of New York Graduate Center course, Bilingual/Polyglot Writers.

13. SPECIAL BILINGUALS

1. Of course, sign language interpreters also change modality, going from an oral language to a sign language or vice versa.
2. Personal communication.
3. George Millar, *Maquis: The French Resistance at War* (London: Cassell, 1945).
4. Sarah Helm, *A Life in Secrets: The Story of Vera Atkins and the Lost Agents of SOE* (London: Abacus, 2006).

14. IN AND OUT OF BILINGUALISM

1. Werner Leopold, *Speech Development in a Bilingual Child* (New York: AMS Press, 1970).
2. From François Grosjean, *Life with Two Languages: An Introduction to Bilingualism* (Cambridge, Mass.: Harvard University Press, 1982), 177.
3. From R. Andersson, "Philosophical Perspectives on Bilingual Education," in Bernard Spolsky and Robert Cooper, eds., *Frontiers of Bilingual Education* (Rowley, Mass.: Newbury House, 1977); reprinted in Grosjean, *Life with Two Languages,* 177.
4. Carroll Barber, "Trilingualism in an Arizona Yaqui village," in Paul Turner, ed., *Bilingualism in the Southwest* (Tucson: University of Arizona Press, 1973), 295–318.
5. Mohamed Abdulaziz-Mkilifi, "Triglossia and Swahili-English Bilingualism in Tanzania," in Joshua Fishman, ed., *Advances in the Study of Societal Multilingualism* (The Hague: Mouton, 1978), 129–152.
6. Marie-Paule Maurer, "Létitia, d'origine portugaise, à l'école luxembourgeoise," *Education et Sociétés Plurilingues* 24 (2008): 81–92.
7. Eva Hoffman, *Lost in Translation* (New York: Penguin, 1989), 104–105.

8. Robbins Burling, "Language Development of a Garo and English Speaking Child," in Evelyn Hatch, ed., *Second Language Acquisition* (Rowley, Mass.: Newbury House, 1978).

9. Ibid., 74.

10. The case of Stephen makes one think of President Barack Obama, who spent four years in Indonesia between the ages of six and ten. He attended a local school and had Indonesian friends. He became relatively fluent in Indonesian (Bahasa Indonesia) but stopped using it with anyone when he returned to the United States, with the exception of his half sister. It is said that he can still hold a general conversation in Indonesian.

11. Lily Wong Fillmore, "Loss of Family Languages: Should Educators Be Concerned?" *Theory into Practice* 39 (2000): 203–210; quotation on 205.

12. Annick De Houwer, *Two or More Languages in Early Childhood: Some General Points and Practical Recommendations* (Washington, D.C.: Center for Applied Linguistics, 1999).

13. Ibid.

14. Grosjean, *Life with Two Languages,* 106.

15. Ibid., 15. Even though this testimony is not recent, things have not changed since then.

16. Richard Rodriguez, *Hunger of Memory: The Education of Richard Rodriguez* (New York: Bantam, 1983), 29.

15. ACQUIRING TWO LANGUAGES

1. Unfortunately, no good statistics exist on this point. Barbara Zurer Pearson and Sylvia Fernández report that among the Hispanic population in Miami, between 6 percent and 15 percent of bilinguals had learned their two languages from birth. Pearson and Fernández, "Patterns of Interaction in the Lexical Growth in Two Languages of Bilingual Infants and Toddlers," *Language Learning* 44 (1994): 617–653.

2. D. Kimbrough Oller et al., "Development of Precursors to Speech in Infants Exposed to Two Languages," *Journal of Child Language* 24 (1997): 407-425.
3. See, for example, Tracey Burns et al., "The Development of Phonetic Representation in Bilingual and Monolingual Infants," *Applied Psycholinguistics* 28 (2007): 455-474.
4. Laura Bosch and Núria Sebastián-Gallés, "Simultaneous Bilingualism and the Perception of a Language-Specific Vowel Contrast in the First Year of Life," *Language and Speech* 46 (2003): 217-243.
5. Anna-Beth Doyle, Mireille Champagne, and Norman Segalowitz report that the average child's age for speaking the first word, as recalled by mothers, is 11.2 months for bilinguals and 11.6 for monolinguals. Doyle, Champagne, and Segalowitz, "Some Issues in the Assessment of Linguistic Consequences of Early Bilingualism," in Michel Paradis, ed., *Aspects of Bilingualism* (Columbia, S.C.: Hornbeam, 1978), 13-20.
6. Personal communication, 13 March 2008. I thank Barbara Zurer Pearson for this information. Her recent book deals at length with the issues discussed; see Barbara Zurer Pearson, *Raising a Bilingual Child* (New York: Random House, 2008).
7. Pearson and Fernández, "Patterns of Interaction."
8. Werner Leopold, *Speech Development in a Bilingual Child* (New York: AMS Press, 1970).
9. Virginia Volterra and Traute Taeschner, "The Acquisition and Development of Language by Bilingual Children," *Journal of Child Language* 5 (1978): 311-326.
10. Coral Bergman, "Interference vs. Independent Development in Infant Bilingualism," in Gary Keller, Richard Teschner, and Silva Viera, eds., *Bilingualism in the Bicentennial and Beyond* (New York: Bilingual Press/Editorial Bilingüe, 1976), 86-96; quotation on 88.
11. Jürgen Meisel, "The Bilingual Child," in Tej Bhatia and William Ritchie, eds., *The Handbook of Bilingualism* (Oxford: Blackwell, 2004), 91-113.

12. Virginia Yip and Stephen Matthews, *The Bilingual Child: Early Development and Language Contact* (Cambridge: Cambridge University Press, 2007).

13. Barry McLaughlin, *Myths and Misconceptions about Second Language Learning: What Every Teacher Needs to Unlearn* (Washington, D.C.: Center for Applied Linguistics, 1993).

14. Catherine Snow and Marianne Hoefnagel-Hohle, "The Critical Period for Language Acquisition: Evidence from Second Language Learning," *Child Development* 49 (1978): 1114-1128.

15. Note that many of these factors also hold for adults, with the exception of school, of course, and family to some extent. It is clear that additional aspects also play a role where adults are concerned.

16. Lily Wong Fillmore, "Second-Language Learning in Children: A Model of Language Learning in Context," in Ellen Bialystok, ed., *Language Processing in Bilingual Children* (Cambridge: Cambridge University Press, 1991), 49-69.

17. Lily Wong Fillmore, "The Second Time Around: Cognitive and Social Strategies in Second-Language Acquisition," Ph.D. diss., Stanford University, 1976.

18. Ibid.

19. Ibid.

20. Jim Cummins, "BICS and CALP: Empirical and Theoretical Status of the Distinction," in Brian Street and Nancy Hornberger, eds., *Encyclopedia of Language and Education,* vol. 2: *Literacy* (New York: Springer Science, 2008), 71-83.

21. Jim Cummins, "Promoting Literacy in Multilingual Contexts," *What Works? Research into Practice,* Research Monograph no. 5, Literacy and Numeracy Secretariat, Ontario (June 2007), 1-4. I will come back to these questions, notably that of biliteracy, in Chapter 19. A complete review of the literacy question can be found in Diane August and Timothy Shanahan, eds., *Developing Literacy in Second-Language Learners: Report of the National Literacy Panel on Lan-*

guage Minority Children and Youth (Mahwah, N.J.: Lawrence Erlbaum, 2006).

16. LINGUISTIC ASPECTS OF CHILDHOOD BILINGUALISM

1. Melania Mikeš, "Acquisition des catégories grammaticales dans le langage de l'enfant," *Enfance* 20 (1967): 289-298.
2. Marilyn Vihman, "The Acquisition of Morphology by a Bilingual Child: A Whole-Word Approach," paper presented at the Fifth Annual Conference on Language Development, Boston University, 1980.
3. Robbins Burling, "Language Development of a Garo and English Speaking Child," in Evelyn Hatch, ed., *Second Language Acquisition* (Rowley, Mass.: Newbury House, 1978).
4. Paul Kinzel, *Lexical and Grammatical Interference in the Speech of a Bilingual Child* (Seattle: University of Washington Press, 1964).
5. Alvino Fantini, "Bilingual Behavior and Social Cues: Case Studies of Two Bilingual Children," in Michel Paradis, ed., *Aspects of Bilingualism* (Columbia, S.C.: Hornbeam, 1978), 283-301.
6. Elizabeth Lanza, "Can Bilingual Two-Year-Olds Code-Switch?" *Journal of Child Language* 19 (1992): 633-658.
7. Erica McClure, "Aspects of Code-Switching in the Discourse of Bilingual Mexican-American Children," Technical Report no. 44, Center for the Study of Reading, University of Illinois at Urbana-Champaign, 1977.
8. Cristina Banfi, "Translation and the Bilingual Child," *Bilingual Family Newsletter* 25 (2008): 1-6.
9. Fred Genesee, Elena Nicoladis, and Johanne Paradis, "Language Differentiation in Early Bilingual Development," *Journal of Child Language* 22 (1995): 611-631.
10. Brian Harris and Bianca Sherwood, "Translating as an Innate Skill," in David Gerver and H. Wallace Sinaiko, eds., *Language Interpretation and Communication* (New York: Plenum, 1978), 155-170.

11. Ibid.

12. François Grosjean, *Life with Two Languages: An Introduction to Bilingualism* (Cambridge, Mass.: Harvard University Press, 1982), 201.

13. Paul Preston, *Mother Father Deaf* (Cambridge, Mass.: Harvard University Press, 1995), 86.

14. Ibid., 145.

15. Ibid., 165.

16. Marguerite Malakoff and Kenji Hakuta, "Translation Skill and Metalinguistic Awareness in Bilinguals," in Ellen Bialystok, ed., *Language Processing in Bilingual Children* (New York: Cambridge University Press, 1991), 141–166.

17. Guadalupe Valdés, *Expanding Definitions of Giftedness: The Case of Young Interpreters from Immigrant Communities* (Mahwah, N.J.: Lawrence Erlbaum, 2003).

18. Fantini, "Bilingual Behavior and Social Cues."

19. Yves Gentilhomme, "Expérience autobiographique d'un sujet bilingue Russe-Français: Prolégomènes théoriques," paper presented at the Third International Conference on Languages in Contact, Justus-Liebig University, Giessen, Germany, 1980.

20. Banfi, "Translation and the Bilingual Child."

17. FAMILY STRATEGIES AND SUPPORT

1. Einar Haugen, "The Stigmata of Bilingualism," in Anwar Dil, ed., *The Ecology of Language: Essays by Einar Haugen* (Stanford: Stanford University Press, 1972), 307–324; quotation on 307.

2. Annick De Houwer, "Parental Language Input Patterns and Children's Bilingual Use," *Applied Psycholinguistics* 28 (2007): 411–424.

3. François Grosjean, *Life with Two Languages: An Introduction to Bilingualism* (Cambridge, Mass.: Harvard University Press, 1982), 171.

4. Susanne Döpke, "Raising Children Bilingually: Some Suggestions for Parents" (1996); this article is available online at www.bilingualoptions.com.au; quotation on 2.

5. Richard Rodriguez, *Hunger of Memory: The Education of Richard Rodriguez* (New York: Bantam Books, 1983).

6. Ray Castro, "Shifting the Burden of Bilingualism: The Case for Monolingual Communities," *Bilingual Review/La Revista Bilingüe* 3 (1976): 3-28; quotations on 5, 8.

7. Grosjean, *Life with Two Languages,* 163.

8. Stephen Caldas and Suzanne Caron-Caldas, "A Sociolinguistic Analysis of the Language Preferences of Adolescent Bilinguals: Shifting Allegiances and Developing Identities," *Applied Linguistics* 23 (2002): 490-514.

9. Nancy Huston, *Losing North: Musings on Land, Tongue and Self* (Toronto: McArthur, 2002), 58.

18. EFFECTS OF BILINGUALISM ON CHILDREN

1. Simon S. Laurie, *Lectures on Language and Linguistic Method in the School* (Cambridge: Cambridge University Press, 1890), 15.

2. Otto Jespersen, *Language* (London: Allen and Unwin, 1922), 148.

3. David Saer, "The Effect of Bilingualism on Intelligence," *British Journal of Psychology* 14 (1923): 25-38. W. Jones and W. Stewart, "Bilingualism and Verbal Intelligence," *British Journal of Psychology* 4 (1951): 3-8. Natalie Darcy, "The Effect of Bilingualism upon the Measurement of the Intelligence of Children of Preschool Age," *Journal of Educational Psychology* 37 (1946): 21-44.

4. Einar Haugen, "The Stigmata of Bilingualism," in Anwar Dil, ed., *The Ecology of Language: Essays by Einar Haugen* (Stanford: Stanford University Press, 1972), 307-324; quotation on 307.

5. Elizabeth Peal and Wallace Lambert, "The Relation of Bilingualism to Intelligence," *Psychological Monographs* 76, no. 27 (1962): 1-23.

6. Merrill Swain and Jim Cummins, "Bilingualism, Cognitive Functioning and Education," *Language Teaching and Linguistics: Abstracts* 12 (1979): 4-18.

7. G. L. MacNab, "Cognition and Bilingualism: A Reanalysis of Studies," *Linguistics* 17 (1979): 231-255.

8. Swain and Cummins, "Bilingualism, Cognitive Functioning and Education."

9. Barry McLaughlin, *Second-Language Acquisition in Childhood* (Hillsdale, N.J.: Lawrence Erlbaum, 1978), quotation on 206.

10. I wish to thank Ellen Bialystok for her guidance through this rather complex field.

11. Ellen Bialystok and Lili Senman, "Executive Processes in Appearance-Reality Tasks: The Role of Inhibition of Attention and Symbolic Representation," *Child Development* 75 (2004): 562–579.

12. Ellen Bialystok, Michelle Martin, and Mythili Viswanathan, "Bilingualism across the Lifespan: The Rise and Fall of Inhibitory Control," *International Journal of Bilingualism* 9 (2005): 103–119.

13. Ellen Bialystok, "Metalinguistic Aspects of Bilingual Processing," *Annual Review of Applied Linguistics* 21 (2001): 169–181.

14. Ibid.

15. Ellen Bialystok and Xiaojia Feng, "Language Proficiency and Its Implications for Monolingual and Bilingual Children," in A. Durgunoglu, ed., *Challenges for Language Learners in Language and Literacy* (New York: Guilford, forthcoming).

16. Ibid.

17. Susanne Döpke, "Understanding Bilingualism and Language Disorder" (2006); this article is available online at www.bilingualoptions.com.au.

18. Johanne Paradis et al., "French-English Bilingual Children with SLI: How Do They Compare with Their Monolingual Peers?" *Journal of Speech, Language, and Hearing Research* 46 (2003): 113–127.

19. Johanne Paradis, "Bilingual Children with Specific Language Impairment: Theoretical and Applied Issues," *Applied Psycholinguistics* 28 (2007): 551–564.

19. EDUCATION AND BILINGUALISM

1. *UNESCO Universal Declaration on Cultural Diversity* (Paris: UNESCO, 2002), objective no. 6, p. 15.

2. Jim Cummins, "Promoting Literacy in Multilingual Contexts," *What Works? Research into Practice*, Research Monograph no. 5, Literacy and Numeracy Secretariat, Ontario (June 2007), 1-4.

3. Quoted in François Grosjean, *Life with Two Languages: An Introduction to Bilingualism* (Cambridge, Mass.: Harvard University Press, 1982), 209.

4. Jacques Levy, *Cesar Chavez: Autobiography of La Causa* (New York: Norton, 1975), 24.

5. Grosjean, *Life with Two Languages*, 211.

6. Cummins, "Promoting Literacy."

7. Richard Rodriguez, *Hunger of Memory: The Education of Richard Rodriguez* (New York: Bantam Books, 1983), 28.

8. Lily Wong Fillmore, "English Learners and Mathematics Learning: Language Issues to Consider," in Alan H. Schoenfeld, ed., *Assessing Mathematical Proficiency* (Cambridge: Cambridge University Press, 2007), 333-344.

9. Maria Brisk, "Bilingual Education," in Bernard Spolsky, ed., *Concise Encyclopedia of Educational Linguistics* (Oxford: Pergamon, 1999), 311-315.

10. I realize that it is not always possible for schools to promote bilingualism in the school language and another language that may be quite rare, especially without the appropriate resources (funds, teachers, educational materials, and so on). That said, it is important to review the ways in which some schools do foster bilingualism among their students, because encouraging the learning and use of languages (publicly and privately) does seem to be the road that lies ahead, at least in many parts of our world. Interested readers may want to refer to Colin Baker, *Foundations of Bilingual Education and Bilingualism* (Clevedon, U.K.: Multilingual Matters, 2006).

11. Michael Krauss, "The Condition of Native North American Languages: The Need for Realistic Assessment and Action," *International Journal of the Sociology of Language* 132 (1998): 9-21.

12. Teresa McCarty, "Revitalising Indigenous Languages in Homogenising Times," *Comparative Education* 39 (2003): 147–163.

13. Wayne Holm, "The 'Goodness' of Bilingual Education for Native American Children," in Teresa McCarty and Ofelia Zepeda, eds., *One Voice, Many Voices: Recreating Indigenous Language Communities* (Tempe and Tucson: Arizona State University Center for Indian Education and University of Arizona American Indian Language Development Institute, 2006), 1–46; quotation on 41–42.

14. Some of this information comes from Professor Maria Brisk, and my thanks go to her; for more information, see the Amigos School Web page, www.cpsd.us/AMI.

15. Cheryl Dressler and Michael Kamil, "First- and Second-Language Literacy," in Diane August and Timothy Shanahan, eds., *Developing Literacy in Second-Language Learners: Report of the National Literacy Panel on Language Minority Children and Youth* (Mahwah, N.J.: Lawrence Erlbaum, 2006), 197–238. I wish to thank Timothy Shanahan for making the report available to me and for answering my questions.

16. For more on biliteracy, see Ellen Bialystok, Gigi Luk, and Ernest Kwan, "Bilingualism, Biliteracy, and Learning to Read: Interactions among Languages and Writing Systems," *Scientific Studies of Reading* 9 (2005): 43–61.

17. The European Schools, which cater to the children of European Union officials as well as local children, represent another model of education favoring bilingualism and multilingualism. According to Alex Housen, in 2002 some 17,000 children, representing fifty nationalities and more than thirty different languages, were enrolled in the ten schools spread across the European Union; see Housen, "Processes and Outcomes in the European Schools Model of Multilingual Education," *Bilingual Research Journal* 26 (2002): 45–64.

Index

Abutalebi, Jubin, 66

Accent: well-known people with accents, 77-78, 83-84; reasons for, 78; characteristics of, 78-79; in a third or fourth language, 80; age limit for, 80; disadvantages of, 81-83; advantages of, 83-84

Acculturation, 111

Acquisition of languages, simultaneous, 178-184, 261n1; case studies, 164, 180-181; main milestones, 179-180; compared with monolingual acquisition, 179-180; one-system position, 181-182; blends and compounds, 181-182; dual-system position, 182-183; differentiating each language, 183; person-language bond, 183-184; dominance, 192

Acquisition of languages, successive, 184-190; the younger, the better myth, 185-186; Wong Fillmore's model, 186-188; strategies in, 187-188; diversity of learners, 189; types of proficiency, 189-190; dominance, 192-193

Activation and deactivation of languages. *See* Language mode

Amigos School, 239-240

Attentional control, 95-96, 223-224, 225

Attitudes: toward bilingualism, 97-107, 176-177; of monolinguals toward bilinguals, 105-107; toward languages, 175

Barber, Carroll, 44, 166

Base language, 27, 39, 40, 41, 43-50, 52, 53, 57, 58, 59-60, 64, 67, 71, 73, 197, 199. *See also* Language choice

Beaujour, Elizabeth, 84, 138, 139-140, 142, 143

Beckett, Samuel, 76, 138, 142

Bergman, Coral, 182

Bialystok, Ellen, 94-95, 223-226

Biel/Bienne, 7, 241

Biculturalism: general aspects of, 27; description of, 109-110, 255n1. *See also* Bicultural people

Bicultural people: characteristics of, 109-110; blending component in, 109-110, 113-114; cultural dominance, 110-111, 119; and immigration, 111; becoming bicultural, 111; acting biculturally, 112-115; cultural modes, 112-115; and identity, 116-120, 124-127, 256n8; attitudes toward, 117

Bilingual, meanings of, 3

Bilingualism: definitions of, 4, 22; and well-learned behaviors, 33-34;

271